Cambridge Elements

Elements in the Philosophy of Science
edited by
Jacob Stegenga
NTU Singapore

UNDERDETERMINATION AND THEORETICAL VIRTUES

Dana Tulodziecki
Purdue University

Shaftesbury Road, Cambridge CB2 8EA, United Kingdom

One Liberty Plaza, 20th Floor, New York, NY 10006, USA

477 Williamstown Road, Port Melbourne, VIC 3207, Australia

314–321, 3rd Floor, Plot 3, Splendor Forum, Jasola District Centre, New Delhi – 110025, India

103 Penang Road, #05-06/07, Visioncrest Commercial, Singapore 238467

Cambridge University Press is part of Cambridge University Press & Assessment, a department of the University of Cambridge.

We share the University's mission to contribute to society through the pursuit of education, learning and research at the highest international levels of excellence.

www.cambridge.org
Information on this title: www.cambridge.org/9781009547833

DOI: 10.1017/9781009278478

© Dana Tulodziecki 2025

This publication is in copyright. Subject to statutory exception and to the provisions of relevant collective licensing agreements, with the exception of the Creative Commons version the link for which is provided below, no reproduction of any part may take place without the written permission of Cambridge University Press & Assessment.

An online version of this work is published at doi.org/10.1017/9781009278478 under a Creative Commons Open Access license CC-BY-NC 4.0 which permits re-use, distribution and reproduction in any medium for non-commercial purposes providing appropriate credit to the original work is given and any changes made are indicated. To view a copy of this license visit https://creativecommons.org/licenses/by-nc/4.0

When citing this work, please include a reference to the DOI 10.1017/9781009278478

First published 2025

A catalogue record for this publication is available from the British Library

ISBN 978-1-009-54783-3 Hardback
ISBN 978-1-009-27844-7 Paperback
ISSN 2517-7273 (online)
ISSN 2517-7265 (print)

Cambridge University Press & Assessment has no responsibility for the persistence or accuracy of URLs for external or third-party internet websites referred to in this publication and does not guarantee that any content on such websites is, or will remain, accurate or appropriate.

For EU product safety concerns, contact us at Calle de José Abascal, 56, 1°, 28003 Madrid, Spain, or email eugpsr@cambridge.org

Underdetermination and Theoretical Virtues

Elements in the Philosophy of Science

DOI: 10.1017/9781009278478
First published online: June 2025

Dana Tulodziecki
Purdue University
Author for correspondence: Dana Tulodziecki, dtulodzi@purdue.edu

Abstract: This Element advances a novel view – the Epistemic Labour View – about the role, limits, and potential of the theoretical virtues as the arbiters of various versions of underdetermination. A central focus is to go beyond the often abstract discussions in this area and to show how the theoretical virtues can illuminate and resolve issues surrounding actual cases of underdetermination found in scientific practice. This title is also available as Open Access on Cambridge Core.

Keywords: underdetermination, theoretical virtues, scientific realism, epistemic virtues, nonempirical virtues, virtues in science, empirically equivalent theories

© Dana Tulodziecki 2025

ISBNs: 9781009547833 (HB), 9781009278447 (PB), 9781009278478 (OC)
ISSNs: 2517-7273 (online), 2517-7265 (print)

Contents

Introduction   1

1 Underdetermination   5

2 Theoretical Virtues   23

3 The Epistemic Labour View of Theoretical Virtues   37

4 Theoretical Virtues and Underdetermination   51

References   69

Introduction

Science is widely regarded as providing one of our best, most secure, and dependable kinds of empirical knowledge. Yet, much of this knowledge involves events, processes, mechanisms, and entities that go beyond the limits of what we can directly observe. Consequently, there is a lively debate about the epistemic status of such unobservables and when and under what circumstances (if any) we are justified in believing claims involving them. According to a rather bleak view about scientific knowledge, we aren't – and never can be – justified in believing such claims. The argument from underdetermination is one of the main arguments that proponents of the bleak view appeal to. Its basic underlying idea is that empirical evidence alone can never single out a particular scientific claim, hypothesis, or theory, since – so the argument goes – there are always competing and incompatible claims that are empirically equivalent, that is, that can also account for the very same observable evidence. As a result, the evidence alone can never point to one of these many competitors as superior to the others: they are underdetermined by the available empirical evidence.

Looking back at the history of science, there are many examples of scientific theories that were underdetermined at one time or another but in which this underdetermination was eventually settled by new evidence. A noteworthy example is the seventeenth-century rivalry between the particle and wave theories of light. As the French theoretical physicist Pierre Duhem (1861–1916) put it, there were "two hypotheses concerning the nature of light; for Newton, Laplace, or Biot light consisted of projectiles hurled with extreme speed, but for Huygens, Young, or Fresnel light consisted of vibrations whose waves are propagated within an ether" (Duhem 1954: 189). According to Newton, light was composed of tiny particles called 'corpuscles' and travelled in straight lines. According to Hooke and Huygens, light was a wave phenomenon in a continuous medium called the 'ether'. The particle and wave theories of light gave competing explanations for a number of optical phenomena such as refraction, and the tie between these two theories was not broken until almost a hundred years later, through the famous white spot experiment (Worrall 1989). Speaking of more recent science, Fraser (2009) has argued that the different variants of quantum field theory are empirically equivalent and therefore underdetermined by the available evidence. Similarly, it has been argued that our current empirical evidence is compatible with different interpretations of the quantum mechanical formalism and that "it is [thus] difficult to justify any one of them as unambiguously supporting specific realist commitments towards unobservable aspects of quantum reality" (Egg & Saatsi 2021: 2).

Underdetermination is not confined to scientific scenarios – it is also prevalent in everyday life and can in principle be applied to anything that involves claims that go beyond the limits of direct observability. For example, the motive of a crime might be underdetermined even after thorough investigation or the cause of a headache might be underdetermined even after extensive evidence gathering, leaving several possible diagnoses. More topically (and worryingly), conspiracy theories also often rely on the idea that evidence underdetermines theories. For example, it has been proposed that the moon landing did not really happen but was an elaborate hoax in which NASA and the U.S. government faked photographs, astronaut testimonies, lunar samples, and other evidence. Climate sceptics have argued against the claim that human activities (burning of fossil fuels, greenhouse gas emissions, and so on) are a major contributor to climate change, proposing instead that non-anthropogenic factors, such as solar flares or natural climate variability, could also entail the observable evidence about how the climate is changing. More recently, conspiracy theorists have claimed that 5G networks are linked to the spread of COVID-19, or even that COVID-19 vaccines contain tracking microchips enabled by 5G technology. Underlying these claims is the shared idea that these conspiracy theories, too, entail the relevant observable evidence and that, therefore, these theories are somehow on a par with 'real' scientific theories, since the evidence fails to uniquely single out the scientific theory over its conspiratorial counterparts. We should note off the bat that even though in these cases the existing evidence is *compatible* with (elaborately enough designed) hoax claims, the scientific evidence is still decisively and conclusively on the side of the moon landing, anthropogenic climate change, and the absence of a link between COVID-19 (vaccines) and 5G technology: in order to hold on to these conspiracy claims, their advocates have to put a lot of work into misinterpreting evidence and scientific support relations. Such cases also make clear that the mere entailing of the observable evidence, or simple compatibility with the observable evidence, is not enough to produce serious rivals to our scientific theories, even if, with sufficient effort, one can technically get them to check off an underdetermination box in the broadest sense.

We can already see that these different kinds of cases raise many questions: What different types of underdetermination are there? What kinds of underdetermination should we be particularly concerned about in science? How do we know when we should regard a particular claim as a serious rival? When and on what grounds can we exclude possible competitors? And can we do so in a principled way that doesn't rely on circular or retroactive reasoning that simply favours antecedently held conclusions? Most importantly: does underdetermination really threaten scientific knowledge?

In this Element, I seek to answer these questions while aiming to restore a more optimistic picture of the scientific enterprise than the bleak view suggests; a picture according to which scientists have at their disposal a rich variety of resources that guide them in their scientific decision-making, and that is, contrary to the bleak view, not just legitimate, but fruitful. The particular candidates I will focus on in this Element and specifically in response to underdetermination are the so-called theoretical virtues. Theoretical virtues, broadly speaking, are properties of our scientific theories such as explanatory power, unifying power, scope, coherence with other scientific theories, consilience, the ability to make novel predictions, parsimony, lack of ad hoc features, fruitfulness, and so on. Appealing to these theoretical virtues in response to underdetermination has been a prominent strategy. It relies on the idea that theories that possess the virtues are more likely to be true than theories lacking them and that therefore the virtues play an epistemic role and can break ties in cases of underdetermination. But this claim is highly controversial: others think that while the virtues might help scientists choose one theory over others, any such choice would rest on pragmatic instead of epistemic reasons. Attitudes towards underdetermination and the theoretical virtues tend to go hand in hand: those who think that underdetermination is a threat to scientific knowledge also think that the virtues can play at best a pragmatic role, whereas those who reject underdetermination as a serious worry hold that the virtues possess epistemic power.

In this Element, I will stake out a new position with respect to underdetermination and the virtues. This position will reject the aforementioned dichotomy and divorce views on the theoretical virtues and on underdetermination from each other. It seeks to relocate discussions of the virtues to the empirical level and argues that, while sometimes the virtues are capable of breaking underdetermination ties on epistemic grounds, they don't engender any kind of in-principle epistemic power that always allows them to do so. In particular, I show that a common argument, according to which theories having theoretical virtues are epistemically superior to theories that lack them, doesn't do much to resolve cases of underdetermination. Even if this argument were to go through, it would be at most a Pyrrhic victory, since in real science this situation – in which one theory has the virtues and its rivals lack them – doesn't arise. In fact, I will argue that this is exactly what we should expect: real scientific controversies are serious precisely because all contenders on the table are genuine rivals, and this involves possessing and putting to work the theoretical virtues as well as other properties we tend to commonly think of as the hallmarks of good science. Thus, general in-principle arguments relying on only one theory exhibiting the virtues over its competitors turn out to be epistemically impotent when taking into account the actual practice of science. As we'll see, it's also this feature that differentiates scientific claims, hypotheses, and theories from those resting on conspiracies and pseudoscience more generally. Combining these various elements, I develop the 'Epistemic Labour View of Theoretical Virtues'. This is grounded in pluralism about the epistemic goals of science and its core claim is that the theoretical virtues play an epistemic role in our scientific theories just in case they work to promote a theory's scientific epistemic goals. The result is a view that allows for the virtues being epistemic without being truth-conducive, contra the two main positions in the virtues debate.

The structure of this Element is as follows. In Section 1, I'll begin by framing the underdetermination argument in its current setting: the debate between scientific realists and anti-realists. In this section, I'll provide some relevant background and explain the main issues that underlie debates about underdetermination, the role that the underdetermination argument plays in the contemporary scientific realism debate, and an overview of the main arguments for and against underdetermination. A further goal is to get a better handle on what the specifically scientific worry about underdetermination is and to distinguish it from more generalized versions with broader domains of applicability.

In Section 2, I set out the debate about the theoretical virtues. Much of this debate has focused on establishing or seeking to undermine the theoretical virtues' connection to truth. This is because one assumption underlying this debate that is common to both proponents and opponents of the virtues' being epistemic is that if one could show that the theoretical virtues are truth-conducive, they would in fact be capable of breaking empirical ties in cases of underdetermination. Contrary to this received view, I'll argue that this is not so: even if there were an agreed-upon list of truth-conducive virtues, I show that this would not resolve actual cases of underdetermination. Moreover, I'll argue that no wholesale or in-principle argument showing that the theoretical virtues are systematically up to their alleged tie-breaking task is possible.

Where does this leave us vis-à-vis the epistemic status of the virtues? In Section 3, I develop the Epistemic Labour View of Theoretical Virtues, based on a liberal pluralism about the epistemic goals of science and a distinction between theories' 'merely having' the virtues and their putting the virtues to work in service of furthering live scientific aims. In Section 4, I'll argue that whether and when the virtues are ultimately epistemic or not is an empirical question that can only be settled by research in the history of science. But, importantly, the epistemic status of the virtues depends not just on the virtues themselves or on whether they are had by particular theories, but also on the context in which they are used. It is a mistake to examine theories in isolation, trying to see whether we can attribute virtues to them while keeping them 'epistemically sequestered'. What role the virtues play is determined not just by whether they are or aren't possessed by particular theories, but also by what live competitors are available, by what questions scientists are trying to answer, by what would count as scientific advancement at that time, and, importantly, by whether the virtues do work in promoting live scientific epistemic goals. This means that while the prospects for general arguments in favour of the theoretical virtues as tie-breakers are dim, the virtues can nevertheless be put to use in underdetermination scenarios, albeit on a case-by-case basis. As a result, sometimes the theoretical virtues manage to break cases of underdetermination and sometimes underdetermination remains. But this is exactly the way things should be, especially during periods of proper scientific debate or controversy which involve real scientific uncertainty. What matters during such periods of knowledge production is that the theories in play are all legitimate scientific contenders and, as this section will show, putting (some of) the theoretical virtues to work in order to promote scientific epistemic goals is one hallmark of this. Section 4 also carves out a new, additional epistemic niche for the theoretical virtues: regardless of whether they are connected to the truth, they have an important epistemic role to play in delineating the boundaries of scientific discourse and in helping scientists address live problems and goals that emerge from the practice of everyday science.

1 Underdetermination

1.1 The Underdetermination Argument

As we have already seen, underdetermination rests on a principled gap between the empirical evidence available for any given hypothesis or theory and the hypothesis or theory itself. From the theoretical side, this gap is impossible to overcome: no matter how good the evidence at hand is, even under the very best circumstances, it will never pick out one particular theory uniquely and instead be compatible with a number of different options (how good these options are is a different matter and one that will be discussed later).

The bulk of contemporary underdetermination discussions in philosophy of science occurs in the debate between scientific realists and scientific anti-realists.[1] Their disagreement is neither metaphysical nor semantic: they both agree that the world is mind-independent and that we should interpret scientific theories literally, both with respect to what they say about the observable and the unobservable. For both of them theoretical scientific terms, such as 'Higgs

---

[1] For an overview of the scientific realism debate, see Chakravartty (2017).

boson', refer and claims involving them (if true) really are about Higgs bosons. The central disagreement between realists and anti-realists is epistemic and centres on when and whether one is justified in believing in the truth, or at least the approximate truth, of our scientific theories. According to scientific realists, we have good reason to believe that our best and most mature theories are indeed (approximately) true, both with respect to what they say about the observable and unobservable. Realists point to the sustained success of our theories as one reason to think so since, they believe, the best explanation for this success is that our theories get things mostly right. Anti-realists deny this. They claim that the success of our scientific theories justifies us only in believing in their ability to 'save the [observable] phenomena' or what some anti-realists, such as van Fraassen, call 'empirical adequacy' (1980: 12). The argument from underdetermination is central to this debate, since it is one of the main anti-realist arguments questioning the scientific realist's commitment to the idea that our best scientific theories are approximately true.[2]

Especially in the context of the scientific realism debate, underdetermination is often argued for in terms of two premises (Kukla 1998, Psillos 1999, Tulodziecki 2017c). The first, sometimes called the 'Empirical Equivalence Thesis', says that for any scientific theory, there are other, logically incompatible, theories that are empirically equivalent to or empirically indistinguishable from the original; that is, there is no empirical data that could discriminate among them. Logical incompatibility is key, since without it the theories under discussion could just be (compatible) variants of each other, without substantial metaphysical differences. The second premise says that entailment of the empirical evidence is the only epistemic criterion that matters when selecting scientific theories or, alternatively, that empirically equivalent theories are equally believable (for more detail on the different formulations of this premise, see 1.3.1). If one accepts these two premises, it follows that we cannot pick scientific theories based on scientific evidence alone. So, if indeed the empirical evidence is the only epistemic basis we have for selecting such theories, this means we have no epistemic or perhaps even rational reasons for selecting the scientific theories we do. And since we tend to think that scientific knowledge is mostly, or perhaps even wholly, comprised of scientific theories, if scientific theories are under threat, so is scientific knowledge. It is because of this that underdetermination has wide-ranging consequences that go beyond esoteric discussions solely of interest to philosophers of science. As we already saw, it can be, and has been, leveraged in support of pseudoscience and conspiracy

---

[2] Underdetermination has also been discussed in other contexts, notably in the debate about science and values (see, for example, Longingo 1990, Intemann 2005, Biddle 2013).

theories. However, as we will see, not all cases of underdetermination are on a par, and different versions of the argument license different conclusions.

It's worth noting explicitly that underdetermination rests on a distinction between the observable and unobservable and that it is because scientific theories involve claims about unobservables that the underdetermination argument can get off the ground. And while it is disputed what exactly should and shouldn't count as observable (Chang 2005, Tulodziecki 2007), it's clear that any scientific theory will involve theoretical or unobservable elements in one form or another. This could be reference to elements that are in principle observable but as of yet unobserved (for example, because they are in the future, possibly the very far future), theoretical elements that are in principle unobservable (perhaps because they are outside our light cone), or elements that are currently unobservable but might one day become observable with further technological or scientific advances. Why should we buy into the underdetermination argument? Let's examine its two premises in a bit more detail.

1.2 Premise 1

According to the Empirical Equivalence Thesis (EET), any theory has logically incompatible rivals that are empirically equivalent to it. In the underdetermination debate, empirically equivalent theories are usually understood to be theories that have the same observational consequence classes or theories that have the same class of empirical models (see, for example, Laudan & Leplin 1991, Okasha 1997: 251).[3] Sometimes, this requirement is put in terms of empirical indistinguishability.[4] Either way, the idea is that two or more theories are empirically equivalent just in case there is no piece of empirical data that could discriminate between them. This situation might be temporary as is often the case when scientific research cannot (yet) produce evidence that could, in principle, distinguish among various competitors. It might also be permanent, as is the case when such potentially discriminatory data is ruled out as a matter of principle, as is arguably the case with at least some of the different interpretations of the quantum-mechanical formalism. In 1.2.1, we'll see a way of turning temporary cases into practically permanent ones, by sequentially modifying theories that are the losers of such 'empirical equivalence duels', in ways that renews their empirical equivalence. It is also worth stressing that, on the standard view of empirical equivalence, theories that are supported by the same *amount* of evidence, but for which the content of this evidence is different, do

---

[3] The former on a syntactic view of theories, the latter on a semantic view. Since these are mostly intertranslatable and none of the arguments in this Element hinge on taking a particular view on scientific theories, my use of 'empirical equivalence' is intended to be neutral between these.

[4] For some different senses of indistinguishability, see Earman (1993).

not count as empirically equivalent. Section 2 will explain how such theories, even in the absence of empirical equivalence, can nevertheless be epistemically equivalent. For now, though, let's focus on what guarantees empirical equivalence. How do we know that empirically equivalent competitors always and really exist for any given theory and that this is not just a matter of luck?

1.2.1 Underdetermination and Holism

One central argument in support of the EET comes from holism about theory-testing. As Duhem already pointed out, theories cannot be tested (or make predictions more generally) in isolation but only holistically, in conjunction with a number of interconnected auxiliary assumptions, including various background theories and experimental initial conditions (1954: 185; see also Ivanova 2021). One consequence of this is that when a theory predicts an experimental result that turns out not to obtain, this cannot conclusively falsify the theory in question. The mistake might lie with the theory itself, but it could also be due to any of the auxiliary assumptions involved. Therefore, such a negative result can only falsify the whole theory-cum-auxiliary complex at once.

This raises questions about what to do when a theory faces empirical problems. One option is to reject the theory, but another is to replace or modify the auxiliaries. Following the latter path might allow scientists to hold on to their original theory even in the face of experimental problems. This might initially strike one as a suspect move, but the history of science is full of examples where this strategy turned out to be exactly right. Indeed, one might view such modifications as part and parcel of the nature of science, which includes continuously refining and revising one's theories as new evidence comes to light – and scientists trying to identify and evaluate specific elements that might be responsible for discrepancies between predictions and observations are just one example of this. For example, one important challenge to Newton's Laws in the early nineteenth century were anomalies in the orbit of Uranus that led to experimental results that deviated from what the Newtonian picture predicted. One line of response to this predicament was to explain these anomalies within the Newtonian framework by modifying the auxiliary assumptions involved in the prediction. This involved postulating the existence of another, hitherto undiscovered planet beyond Uranus that exerted gravitational pull on Uranus, thereby explaining its anomalous orbit. In 1846, Leverrier and Adams independently predicted the existence of such a planet – Neptune – a prediction that was confirmed shortly thereafter by

Galle. In this case, modifying the auxiliaries rather than rejecting Newton's well-entrenched theory turned out to be a good move.

But this is not always the case. Leverrier tried to pursue the same strategy in 1859, albeit unsuccessfully that time. The problematic experimental discrepancy this time centred on the anomalies with Mercury's perihelion, similar to the ones observed earlier in the case of Uranus. Once again, Leverrier tried to predict a new planet. This planet, Vulcan, was hypothesized to be inside Mercury's orbit and small enough to not be easily visible, but just the right size to account for the anomalous rate of the precession of the perihelion in Mercury's orbit. But despite many supposed 'sightings', Vulcan was never found. In this case, adjusting the auxiliaries failed and it was finally accepted that no such planet existed. Newton's theory – successful though it was – was eventually rejected and replaced by Einstein's Theory of General Relativity. This made obsolete the need for an additional planet, since the theory's curved spacetime was sufficient to account for Mercury's observed orbit. However, Einstein's Theory of General Relativity was not experimentally confirmed until 1919 when, during a total solar eclipse, Sir Arthur Eddington observed that the locations of stars during the eclipse appeared displaced due to the sun's gravitational influence, at just the angle that Einstein predicted:[5] starlight was travelling along spacetime paths curved by the sun's gravitational influence (for a detailed account of this episode, including a number of interesting controversies surrounding it, see Kennefick 2021). In the period leading up to Eddington's observation and subsequent confirmation of Einstein's theory, the two available options were underdetermined by the available evidence: Newtonian physics with Vulcan and General Relativity without Vulcan were empirically equivalent and the data left open which was correct.

This case is a good illustration of the way in which Duhem's holism – and different potential resolutions to discrepancies between prediction and observation – supports the first premise of the underdetermination argument. But while it is true that Duhem speculated about the possibilities of modifying the auxiliaries in order to accommodate evidence, he nowhere indicates that he thinks this process is always reasonable. For example, he cites Foucault's experiment which measured the velocity of light in water and air and which was supposed to distinguish between the wave theory of light (predicting that the velocity of light in any medium denser than air is smaller than the velocity of light in air) and the particle theory of light (predicting the opposite). Despite the fact that Foucault's experiment came out in favour of the wave theory of light, according to Duhem, "[i]t would be rash to believe, … that Foucault's

---

[5] Newton also predicted this displacement, but at a different angle.

experiment condemns once and for all the very hypothesis of emission, i.e., the assimilation of a ray of light to a swarm of projectiles. If physicists had attached some value to this task, they would undoubtedly have succeeded in founding on this assumption a system of optics that would agree with Foucault's experiment" (187). Duhem thus acknowledges that it would have been perfectly *possible* to have modified some of the auxiliary assumptions and to hold on to the particle theory of light; however, he also denies that it would have been reasonable to do so. Here Duhem introduces the notion of *le bon sens*, or good sense, which is supposed to guide scientists' rejection and acceptance of theories: "Pure logic is not the only rule for our judgements; certain opinions which do not fall under the hammer of the principle of contradiction are in any case perfectly unreasonable. These motives which do not proceed from logic and yet direct our choices, these "reasons which reason does not know" and which speak to the ample "mind of finesse" but not to the "geometric mind," constitute what is appropriately called good sense" (217).[6] As an example of good sense, Duhem cites Jean Biot, who resolutely defended the particle theory of light through a number of modifications and extensions of the auxiliaries before eventually giving it up in favour of the wave theory.

Thus, Duhem thinks that, in some sense, we can 'refute' individual hypotheses, if, for example, the systems in which they are embedded (Newtonian optics, in this case, or Newton's Laws in the case of Mercury's perihelion) do not represent reality as well as other systems with different postulates (Huygensian optics, in this case, or General Relativity earlier in this subsection). But while Duhem thinks good sense is to be recommended, he also realizes that it does not force us to give up anything and that not everyone is equally possessed of good sense: "it may be that we find it childish and unreasonable for the first physicist to maintain obstinately at any cost, at the price of continual repairs and many tangled-up stays, the worm-eaten columns of a building tottering in every part, when by razing these columns it would be possible to construct a simple, elegant, and solid system. But these reasons of good sense do not impose themselves with the same implacable rigor that the prescriptions of logic do. There is something vague and uncertain about them; they do not reveal themselves at the same time with the same degree of clarity to all minds" (217).

This last quotation points the way towards turning Duhem's holism into a more principled argument for the EET. Given that it is only ever the conjunction of theory and auxiliaries that results in observable consequences, if a theory is not empirically equivalent to another, one can always modify the auxiliaries

---

[6] For more on Duhem and 'good sense', see Ivanova (2014).

of the first until the two holistic theoretical frameworks *are* empirically equivalent. And if further evidence comes along that breaks the tie between these two options, one can make further adjustments until empirical equivalence is achieved once again, and so on. It is because of this that the common distinction between merely temporary cases of underdetermination (that eventually get resolved by new evidence) and permanent ones (that are immune to being resolved by evidence) is not particularly helpful, since the aforementioned strategy can always turn temporary cases of underdetermination into permanent ones – or at least into a continuous and hence effectively permanent succession of temporary ones.

This strategy of generating empirically equivalent rivals – that for Duhem only applied to the "fundamental" sciences (1954: 180)[7] – is taken to the extreme by Quine, who thinks that holism applies not just to any science whatsoever but to any statement, scientific or not, and therefore gives rise to a potentially much more radical form of underdetermination. This is a consequence of how Quine conceives of knowledge in general, illustrated by his image of science or knowledge as a "field of force":

> [T]otal science is like a field of force whose boundary conditions are experience. A conflict with experience at the periphery occasions readjustments on the interior of the field. Truth values have to be redistributed over some of our statements. Revaluation of some statements entails revaluation of others, because of their logical inter-connections – the logical laws being in turn simply certain further statements of the system, certain further elements of the field ... But the total field is so underdetermined by its boundary conditions, experience, that there is much latitude of choice as to what statements to reevaluate in the light of any single contrary experience. (1951: 42–43)

Quine himself is somewhat inconsistent about how radical a version of holism and the resulting underdetermination he holds, stating in *Two Dogmas* that "[t]he unit of empirical significance is the whole of science" (1951: 42) and in *On Empirically Equivalent Systems of the World* that "[l]ittle is gained by saying that the unit is in principle the whole of science, however defensible this claim may be in a legalistic way" (1975: 314–315). Regardless of what version of holism and underdetermination Quine ultimately held, what these passages bring out, and the point I want to emphasize, is that holism comes in degrees, that these degrees correspond to the size of the minimal unit one thinks is necessary for deriving empirical consequences from a theory and that this, in conjunction

---

[7] Duhem restricts his holism to the physical (or "fundamental") sciences, excluding "applied" sciences like physiology or botany to which, he thinks, his thesis does not apply (1954: 180).

with views on what units are potentially up for revision, gives rise to weaker and stronger forms of underdetermination. On one end of the spectrum, we have the relatively modest holism and underdetermination of Duhem which, as we saw, for Duhem applied only to "fundamental sciences" and whose consequences would ideally be reined in by good sense (1954). At the opposite end of the spectrum, we have a type of radical holism and underdetermination, exemplified by Quine in the following famous quotation (regardless of whether he himself ultimately espoused this or not):

> Any statement can be held true come what may, if we make drastic enough adjustments elsewhere in the system. Even a statement very close to the periphery can be held true in the face of recalcitrant experience by pleading hallucination or by amending certain statements of the kind called logical laws. Conversely, by the same token, no statement is immune to revision. Revision even of the logical law of the excluded middle has been proposed as a means of simplifying quantum mechanics; and what difference is there in principle between such a shift and the shift whereby Kepler superseded Ptolemy, or Einstein Newton, or Darwin Aristotle? (1951: 43).[8]

The fact that no statement is – at least in principle – immune to revision is what can occasion radical forms of underdetermination. At the extreme, as Quine tells us, we always have the option of abandoning some laws of logic or pleading hallucinations (43).

What does this relationship between units of holism and radicalness of underdetermination look like more concretely? Let's return for a moment to Foucault's experiment, which showed that light travels more slowly in water than air and thereby supported the wave theory over the particle theory of light. As we know from Duhem, Foucault's experiment did not just test in isolation a particular prediction about how fast light would travel in a medium denser than air (water), but instead its outcomes confronted a much larger holistic unit. In this case, the theoretical complex included a number of interconnected hypotheses and auxiliary and background assumptions about the nature of light, principles of optics, the properties of different testing media, as well as assumptions about the instruments and measurement techniques involved. Foucault's experiment tested this entire, more holistic theoretical framework, pitching against each other the wave and particle theories of light. It is because of this that, even after the results of Foucault's experiment are in, there is underdetermination between, on the one hand, the wave theory as it was and, on the other, a suitably modified version of the particle theory. Someone

---

[8] In *Demystifying Underdetermination*, Laudan (1990) examines Quine's position in some detail; he also disambiguates several other uses of the underdetermination thesis, including those by Lakataos, Feyerabend, Hesse, Bloor, and Collins.

wanting to hold on to a corpuscular view of light instead of adopting the wave theory – even in the face of contradictory experimental evidence – could have proposed any number of modifications. For example, Foucault's experiment involved instruments, including a rotating mirror, that were supposed to measure light speeds with high degrees of accuracy in both air and water, and someone could have questioned the accuracy of Foucault's measurements and/or apparatus. Someone could have also posited that factors other than the nature of light itself influenced the outcome of the experiment, or that light particles undergo behavioural changes when entering denser media. Similarly, it was possible to argue that the existing consensus about the properties of air and water media were mistaken, or to postulate new forces affecting light in different media differently, giving rise to new types of interactions.

Note that while all these strategies go beyond what Duhem considered good sense, they are also still within broadly scientific confines. They don't question, for example, the general laws of physics, or even specific laws, such as Snell's law, which was used to derive the expected behaviour of light in different media; similarly, there is broad consensus about how to conduct scientific experiments, scientific methodology, and so on. A larger holistic unit, including not just competing physical theories but also metaphysical assumptions, could have given rise to more extreme underdetermination: in this spirit, one might now also reject the principle that causes precede their effects, introduce a supernatural intelligence giving light particles consciousness so they can adjust their speed in different media, postulate that light particles experience time dilation when entering water, thereby making them appear slower to us, or suggest that water creates localized distortions of reality around light particles entering it. Taking things further still, one could extend the holistic unit in play once again, so as to include assumptions about social, scientific, and political structures, whose rejection could lead to even more radical underdetermination. One could posit, for example, a full-blown and large-scale conspiracy, in which scientists, institutions, and government agencies conspired to falsify experimental evidence in favour of the wave theory, perhaps because the wave theory challenged traditional French hierarchies of knowledge production and so constituted a better fit with the various Enlightenment values crucial to French liberal thought at the time.

The same point can arise less explicitly and more informally, in contexts in which one is confronted with new information. As a more contemporary example, take someone who is confronted for the first time with the atmospheric phenomenon of contrails, trails of condensed water vapour left by jet engines. After combustion, jet engines emit hot water vapour which subsequently cools and condenses into the Earth's atmosphere and under the right atmospheric conditions, visible condensation trails form. These conditions are most commonly found at planes' cruising altitudes (10,000–13,000 metres) and therefore contrails are most often observed tailing planes. The occurrence, extent, and duration of contrails are determined by local atmospheric conditions, with cold and humid air being favourable for contrails, whereas air that is too dry gives rise to either very short-duration or no contrails at all. When the conditions are just right, the water vapour can turn into ice, giving rise to more persistent contrails and in rarer circumstances, contrails can even appear iridescent. A very different interpretation of contrails, especially of the last two types, involves a conspiracy theory about 'chemtrails'. This holds that contrails, instead of being an atmospheric, scientific phenomenon, are trails containing chemical or biological materials, sprayed intentionally by unknown nefarious agents for purposes ranging from warfare to population control and psychological manipulation. Someone who holds fixed most of their web of belief might make local updates to their scientific beliefs, incorporating new information about atmospheric conditions and cloud physics. Someone who is willing to modify large parts of their web might make substantial revisions not just to their scientific but also to their social and political beliefs, thereby being able to coherently maintain belief in chemtrails. They might reject the meteorology, physics, and chemistry around contrail formation, and start believing that the media, government regulators, scientists, airlines, and environmental groups are all in on the 'contrails sham', lying on behalf of the shadowy powers responsible for the trails.

While all these strategies are psychologically possible, the question is if and when they are reasonable (see also Laudan 1990: 326). Unlike Duhem, Quine gives no prescription as to when any of these strategies are to be legitimately employed. In *Two Dogmas* he acknowledges that, on the whole, we do not resort to anything like abandoning classical logic or pleading hallucination, since doing so would result in systems with increased theoretical complexity. This, however, is merely a pragmatic consideration and not one which seems to have any epistemic import.

However this may be, there are two important points to stress in this discussion. First, the question of what one is willing and unwilling to revise in order to hold on to a certain claim has direct consequences for the resulting form of underdetermination. Second, it's important to be very clear about what exactly is involved in any alleged underdetermination claim and its associated holism. Failure to do so is problematic, because someone might start off by presenting a rather plausible and innocuous version only to then later on draw radical conclusions that do not actually follow from that particular version (see also Laudan 1990).

1.2.2 Algorithms

Another approach to establishing the EET, and one that doesn't involve modifications of existing theories or auxiliaries, is to generate options that replace a whole theory or theoretical system at once, instead of engaging in the kind of piecemeal modifications we just saw. Finding wholesale scientific alternatives to our current scientific theories is generally hard. And while there are examples, they are not exactly plentiful. One notable case of a genuinely scientific example of underdetermination – Newtonian Mechanics with the centre of the universe at absolute rest and while moving at an absolute constant velocity – was introduced into the contemporary literature by van Fraassen (1980, but see also Laudan & Leplin 1991 and Earman 1993). In fact, Newton himself already recognized that "[t]he motions of bodies included in any given space are the same among themselves, whether that space is at rest, or moves uniformly forwards in a right line without any circular motion" (1966: 20). However, since all of these options "involve exactly the same ontology and ideology for space, time, and motion", Earman has argued that "no very interesting form of underdetermination is in the offing" (1993: 31). Earman goes on to provide some cases that he thinks are both more interesting and also "remove the worry that the underdetermination thesis ... is vacuously true because there are no concrete examples of interestingly different but empirically indistinguishable rivals to successful scientific theories" (31). Newtonian mechanics without absolute space "can be opposed by a theory which eschews gravitational force in favour of a non-flat affine connection and which predicts exactly the same particle orbits as TN [Newtonian mechanics] for gravitationally interacting particles" (31). Further and more recent examples have included the different global structures of our cosmological models (Manchak 2009), the variants of quantum field theory (Fraser 2009), different formulations of nineteenth-century electrodynamics (Pietsch 2012), Ptolemaic, Copernican, and Tychonic theories of planetary motion (Miyake 2015), underdetermination of the plasticity-first hypothesis in evolutionary biology (Kovaka 2019), and the various interpretations of quantum mechanics (Egg & Saatsi 2021).[9] Another class of genuine scientific alternatives can be found during periods of theory-change in which one picture of the world gets replaced with another, such as the shift from Ptolemy to Copernicus, from Newton to Einstein, from the miasma to

---

[9] For discussions of whether different scientific domains are prone to underdetermination in the same way, see Cleland 2002, Turner 2005, Dawid 2006, Belot 2015, Currie 2018. Belot's and Dawid's work is concerned with physics, while Cleland, Currie, and Turner focus on the historical sciences. Work emphasizing the latter has been one of the most interesting developments surrounding underdetermination, but since it does not always intersect with the realism debate, I'm foregoing a more detailed discussion here.

the germ theory of disease, from Lamarckism to Darwinian Evolution, or from fixism to continental drift.

Regardless of how these scientific alternatives are generated, however, they are not easy to come by and generating them on demand seems nigh impossible. What's more, even if as a matter of fact such alternatives exist in many cases, there is no guarantee that a scientifically respectable competitor will always be available for any theory whatsoever. They therefore cannot support or guarantee the EET in the same general and in-principle way that the Duhem-Quine line of argument did. It is for this reason that, in the context of establishing the EET, discussions of wholesale 'rivals' have focused on doing so by means of relying on various kinds of algorithms; without them the existence of such rivals cannot be guaranteed. In this vein, Kukla, for example, has argued that algorithms are necessary to make the case for underdetermination and that the only way to establish the EET is "to provide a universal algorithm for constructing rivals from any given theory" (1998: 59).

So, what algorithmic options are on the table? One of the simplest was introduced by van Fraassen (1984): for any given theory, construct a rival by postulating an alternative that claims that the empirical consequences of the original are true, but that the theory itself is false. Slightly more involved options are discussed by Kukla, such as the idea that the world behaves differently when unobserved, but in its usual way when observed (1998), or the fiction that a species of beings creates an exact simulacrum of our universe – including all its observable and unobservable entities – with the one exception that this alternative universe depends on a machine "that is occasionally turned off for maintenance and repair" (1996: 157, 1998: 75–76). Some of these examples veer close to sceptical hypotheses, and even though sceptical hypotheses aren't algorithms as such, they, too, count as one further way in which to establish the EET; after all, they are designed specifically to meet both the EET's requirements, logical incompatibility and empirical equivalence.

One important point to note about such approaches is that the 'rivals' generated in these ways don't target *scientific* knowledge in particular but apply indiscriminately to any kind of empirical knowledge whatsoever. As before, there is a close connection between the kind of 'proof' that is given of the EET and the resulting form of underdetermination. On the one hand, if one's proof of Premise 1 rests on sceptical or algorithmic constructions, the resulting form of underdetermination will be ubiquitous, but not specific to science. This is the only way to establish the EET for good and to guarantee in advance that *any* scientific theory will *always* have at least one empirically equivalent rival. But since such constructions – by design – are general and therefore apply to *all* knowledge and not just scientific knowledge, the resulting underdetermination targets much more than the original underdetermination argument for *scientific* theories by evidence aimed for. Instead of threatening the possibility of scientific knowledge via scientific theories' unobservable parts, it threatens all knowledge, both observable and unobservable. Whichever exact strategy one chooses, as long as the EET is established via an advance guarantee of empirically equivalent rivals, this ubiquitous and general underdetermination will always be a consequence. On the other hand, if your case for Premise 1 is less general, you might get genuinely scientific underdetermination but have to forego an argument that is generally applicable to any scientific theory whatsoever. The more tailored the EET – whether to specific theories, areas of science, or even 'just' scientific knowledge – the less guarantee of empirically equivalent rivals. Thus, the more general and stronger the case for the EET, the less threatening the resulting form of underdetermination to scientific knowledge; the less general and weaker the case for the EET, the more threatening the resulting form of underdetermination to scientific knowledge.

1.2.3 Formulating the EET

In the version of the EET presented at the beginning of this section, I took care to give a neutral formulation that merely talked about the existence of empirically equivalent and logically incompatible rivals, without putting further constraints on those options. So far, we understood empirical equivalence in its most minimal sense of empirical indistinguishability. But many formulations of the EET aren't this neutral and build in particular relationships between theory and evidence. For example, sometimes the EET is stated as "any theory has empirically equivalent rivals that are just as compatible with the evidence as the original", at other times it is formulated as "any theory has empirically equivalent rivals that are supported equally well by the evidence", even though requiring equal support clearly amounts to imposing an additional and independent epistemic constraint. Since such formulations build theory-evidence relations in from the get-go, they might therefore provide more or less plausible or more or less easily established versions of the EET. I deliberately stuck to the neutral version, so as to not to prejudge the issue of potentially controversial support relations, but also because I think it muddies the waters to run together discussions in which the existence of empirically equivalent options is established as a matter of deductive reasoning (such as through the Duhem-Quine line of argument or invoking algorithms) and versions that have particular epistemic requirements about the relationship between theory and evidence built in from the start. This is especially so, because there are many different such relations that could hold and it's an open question which ones are epistemically desirable, which ones are easier or harder to come by, and which ones we might want to require for underdetermination. Moreover, such formulations might be question-begging, since the second premise of the underdetermination argument focuses precisely on the question of epistemic support relations, both with respect to what kind of relationship between theory and evidence is relevant for the argument, but also with respect to whether there are other factors besides the evidence that make an epistemic impact. Before turning to this premise in the next subsection, I wish to emphasize the importance of being aware of what exactly is built into any given version of the two premises individually and into the argument as a whole. In particular, one should be wary of potential entry points for sleights of hand in which a highly plausible proof of the EET – for example, one that merely involves pointing out that empirical equivalents exist – is used as the basis for an inference that it does not in fact license, such as the claim that there are equally well supported empirically equivalent scientific theories. As we are about to see, these amount to very different things.

1.3 Premise 2

1.3.1 Formulating Premise 2 and Theory-Evidence Relations

Let's turn now to the second premise of the underdetermination argument, the one that is supposed to establish that empirical equivalence is sufficient for underdetermination, that is, that nothing else besides the empirical evidence matters (or ought to matter) in choosing scientific theories. We can think of this premise as trying to establish the appropriate parameters of epistemic constraint around theory-choice and then effectively asserting that only the empirical evidence counts in this respect. I'll start out by noting that significantly different versions of this premise exist. For example, Psillos calls Premise 2 the 'Entailment Thesis', formulating it as "the entailment of the evidence is the only epistemic constraint on the confirmation of a theory" (1999: 163). Kukla states it as "empirically equivalent hypotheses are equally believable" (1998: 58). According to Earman, "any observation that provides reason to believe one of the empirically equivalent theories will give equally good reason to believe each of the other theories" (1993: 19). These versions express significantly different claims and much therefore hinges on how exactly this premise is formulated. In order to stay neutral among these formulations, I'll refer to this premise as the 'Epistemic Constraint Thesis', or ECT, from now on. Here are some of the different (positive) relations that can obtain between theories or theoretical systems and empirical evidence, in order of strength (see also Laudan 1990: 329): a theory may be logically compatible with the evidence, logically entail the evidence, explain the evidence, or be empirically supported by the evidence. And where Psillos builds in a merely logical relationship between theory and evidence – entailment – both Kukla's and Earman's versions require the substantially stronger notions of equal believability or equal support. However, as Laudan (Laudan 1990: 329) has pointed out, there is a gap between mere logical relations that might obtain between theories and evidence, such as being compatible with the evidence or logically entailing it, and broader, positive epistemic relations that are more substantial than those of logic alone, such as explanatory or empirical support relations. In particular, "theories may entail statements that they nonetheless do not explain; self-entailment being the most obvious example" and they may also "entail evidence statements, yet not be empirically supported by them (e.g., if the theory was generated by the algorithmic manipulation of the "evidence" in question)" (Laudan 1990: 329). It is unclear whether, with this last statement, Laudan is questioning precisely what is at issue with respect to the second premise. After all, its proponents claim that the entailment of evidence is the only epistemic constraint on theory-choice. Is this supposed to amount to the claim that entailment implies empirical support? Since there are so many different versions of the ECT, I won't settle the issue here but merely point out that a lot hinges on the exact way in which potential theory-evidence relationships are articulated.

Unsurprisingly, what exactly one takes this premise to be has consequences for how ubiquitous and plausible the resulting type of underdetermination is. Entailment of the evidence is easy to come by (as we saw in our discussion of the first premise), and while it has the advantage of generating plenty of cases of underdetermination, one might find it too cheap to generate many cases of genuine scientific interest (Kitcher 1993: 209, 2001: 37). Equal empirical support or believability is much harder to achieve, and while cases that live up to this requirement might be more scientifically plausible (although see below), they will also be fewer (Kitcher 1993: Chapter 7). Thus, as before, it's important, for any given instance of the argument, to pay attention to which version it advances, and for any given case, to understand exactly which version it instantiates.

Generally speaking, though, the ECT seeks to establish the epistemic constraints on theory-choice and we can think of the two premises of the underdetermination argument as seeking to establish empirical and epistemic equivalence respectively. Note that both proponents and detractors of the argument think that epistemic equivalence is required for underdetermination to occur. After all, if there was an epistemic difference among theories, theory-choice wouldn't be underdetermined and one would know how to select one theory over the rest. Yet, the fact that both sides require epistemic equivalence is often obscured by the different formulations of the argument, partially due to the fact that the point of many of the argument's proponents is precisely that epistemic equivalence is no more than empirical equivalence.

1.3.2 Objections to Premise 2

There have been two main lines of criticism against the ECT, both designed to show that epistemic equivalence does not follow from empirical equivalence. The first grants that empirical evidence might be the only epistemic factor in theory choice, but attacks the idea that empirically equivalent theories are equally believable or well supported. The second seeks to establish that there are plenty of factors besides the empirical evidence, for example the theoretical virtues, that are involved in genuine epistemic equivalence.

The locus classicus for the first kind of objection is Laudan and Leplin (1991). As they point out, "the empirical equivalence of a group of rival theories, should it obtain, would not by itself establish that they are underdetermined by the evidence. One of a number of empirically equivalent theories may be uniquely preferable on evidentially probative grounds" (1991: 450). Laudan and Leplin's strategy is to attack the central presupposition of the underdetermination argument, the idea that "if theories possess the same empirical consequences, then they will inevitably be equally well (or ill) supported by those instances" (460). They do so by arguing for two points, "first, that significant evidential support may be provided a theory by results that are not empirical consequences of the theory"; second, "that (even) true empirical consequences need lend no evidential support to a theory" (460).

Let's start with the idea that theories can be supported by claims that are not in their empirical consequence class. In the simplest case, Laudan and Leplin point out, different instances of a universal generalization may lend evidential support to each other, even though they are clearly not empirical consequences of each other (461). More substantially and importantly, they also adduce a number of actual scientific examples from the history of science that firmly establish that hypotheses or theories can be confirmed by statements they don't entail. Their examples all share the same structure and are designed to highlight the scientific importance of indirect support: assume a theory entails two different, independent hypotheses and also that evidence supporting the second hypothesis accumulates. Laudan and Leplin argue that because the second hypothesis is strongly supported, this in turn supports the larger, more general theory of which this hypothesis is a consequence. And, since that more general theory is now more strongly supported, so are that theory's consequences, including the first hypothesis. In this way, evidence for one hypothesis – the second – can indirectly support another – the first – via the theory or larger programme that entails both of them. For example, according to Laudan and Leplin, although Brownian motion is not a consequence of atomic theory, it supported atomic theory via supporting the larger programme that was statistical mechanics (461). The upshot of this and their other examples is that one of a pair of empirically equivalent theories can be supported more strongly than another, even if they both entail the same evidence, because one of the theories may be supported indirectly, just as was the case for atomic theory. Adding a further reason for differential support, Laudan and Leplin cite Maxwell's and Einstein's appeal to analogical reasoning in supporting several of their hypotheses, arguing that "sophisticated analogies can [also] be evidentially probative", even though they don't rely on any entailment relations at all (464). Thus, again, there is more to evidential support than being an empirical consequence, and therefore empirical equivalence is insufficient for epistemic equivalence.

Another objection relies on the idea that being in a theory's empirical consequence class is not enough to furnish that theory with evidential support. In other words, there can be members of a theory's empirical consequence class that do not confirm that theory. To use one of Laudan's and Leplin's own examples: finding that a cold clears up after drinking coffee for several days does not support the hypothesis that coffee cures colds. As they put it, "[n]o philosopher of science is willing to grant evidential status to a result e with respect to a hypothesis H just because e is a consequence of H. That is the point of two centuries of debate over such issues as the independence of e, the purpose for which H was introduced, the additional uses to which H may be put, the relation of H to other theories, and so forth" (466). Moreover, and complementing Laudan and Leplin's line of argument, even in the event in which two theories are confirmed by the very same empirical consequences, these same consequences don't necessarily confirm their respective theories in the same way or to the same degree. Mayo (1997), for example, has argued against underdetermination on the grounds that "more adequate accounts of hypothesis testing ... [get] around the underdetermination challenge" (1997: 243). On Mayo's view, not every test of a hypothesis constitutes a severe test. As a result, even if a number of hypotheses are both empirically equivalent and all tested by the same evidence, they might not all be tested equally severely. In this way, different hypotheses might bear different evidential support relations to the evidence – more support for those hypotheses that are tested severely than those tested non-severely.

But while these responses go some way towards addressing the upshot of the ECT, there are still a number of open questions with respect to how exactly empirical support relations figure into this part of the underdetermination argument. Note also that, although plausible and powerful, Laudan and Leplin's arguments are not without problems. Okasha (1997), for example, has argued that their response to the entailment thesis rests on mutually incompatible principles of confirmation (see Hempel 1945).

So much for the first line of criticism. What about the second? This essentially denies that all there is to epistemic equivalence is empirical equivalence and seeks to establish that, regardless of the issues concerning empirical support relations, there are criteria *besides* the evidence and its relationship to the theory or hypotheses it aims to confirm that also have epistemic relevance for theory-choice. Therefore, even if two theories are supported by the evidence equally well (which, given the issues just discussed, might already be a tall order), this does not mean that both of them are equally good choices. One of them might still be epistemically superior due to other properties, and it thus does not follow even from similar or the same evidential support that theory-choice is underdetermined. It might be underdetermined by the available *evidence* but, opponents of the ECT claim, that is not all that is required for scientific underdetermination: for that to happen, theories need to be *epistemically* equivalent as well. What exactly is involved in epistemic equivalence is, of course, a matter of debate: anti-realists think it's just empirical equivalence; hence their support of the ECT. Realists think there's more to epistemic equivalence than just the observable evidence; hence their rejection of the ECT. While there is no consensus on what exactly these extra ingredients are, the main realist suggestions have centred on the idea of so-called theoretical virtues – properties our various scientific hypotheses and theories might possess and that are capable of conferring epistemic currency on them. What sorts of properties ought to count in this context is controversial, but some popular candidates that have been put forward include coherence with other theories, consilience, scope, unifying power, explanatory power, a theory's not being ad hoc, its being capable of generating novel predictions, fruitfulness, and sometimes elegance and simplicity. Whatever the exact list, the general idea is that these properties make it more likely for theories having them to be true than theories lacking them. This in turns confers an epistemic advantage on theories possessing the virtues and therefore the virtues can single out one theory over others – thus breaking underdetermination, even if those theories are otherwise empirically equivalent and equally well supported by the available evidence.

It should be noted that the debate about the theoretical virtues is whether they are indeed capable of conferring epistemic power on theories possessing them, not on whether they are used in theory-choice as such. Even anti-realists admit that the theoretical virtues can help with theory-choice – they just don't think that choices on this basis are epistemic ones, but instead merely pragmatic ones.

Thus, one of the central debates about the virtues is whether they are solely pragmatic (van Fraassen 1980: 87) or whether they have the connection to (approximate) truth that realists require.[10] Recent responses and discussions of underdetermination have focused mostly on this point; the next section will explore and discuss this issue in more detail.

Before moving on to this discussion, I briefly want to point to a more recent development in the classic underdetermination debate. This is Stanford's (2006) Problem of Unconceived Alternatives, which, he argues, is a problem for realists even abandoning empirical equivalence as a requirement for underdetermination and accepting their more inclusive view of evidence. Stanford makes his case by drawing on the history of science, arguing that we have systematically failed at conceiving alternatives to our best scientific theories that were significantly different but just as well confirmed by the available evidence at the time. Since, according to Stanford, we have done this throughout history, we therefore have no reason to think that our current theories are any different or any better. The result is a version of underdetermination, questioning the view that our evidence is capable of singling out our best confirmed theories over others – just that the other options in his case are unconceived alternatives, not empirically equivalent current ones. With respect to the theoretical virtues, Stanford's unconceived alternatives are on a par with the competitors raised in more traditional underdetermination scenarios. Since my arguments in the remainder of this Element don't rely on empirical equivalence as a condition for underdetermination, they can – with minor modifications to account for unconceivedness – be applied equally well to Stanford-type cases and so I'll forgo discussing them separately. Let us turn to those arguments next.

2 Theoretical Virtues

2.1 Introduction

The idea behind the theoretical virtues response to the second premise of the underdetermination argument is that the virtues can function as potential tiebreakers in underdetermination scenarios. One important obstacle to establishing that the virtues could function in this capacity, however, is doing so in a way that is acceptable to anti-realists; otherwise, one is just begging the antirealist question. The good news for anyone embarking on this endeavour is that it's not necessary to establish the full-blown truth-conduciveness of the

---

[10] There is also some discussion about the aesthetic dimensions of the theoretical virtues (see, for example, McAllister 1999 and Ivanova 2017). It is currently an open question to what extent this maps onto the epistemic/pragmatic distinction with respect to underdetermination and in the scientific realism debate more generally.

virtues: anti-realists are interested in defeating all forms of realism and since the argument from underdetermination rests on an in-principle point about the virtues not being capable of playing an epistemic role, realists can make significant headway by trying to undercut this in-principle claim. The bad news is that doing so in a general and systematic way will turn out not to work in the realists' favour, as I'll show in this section. More optimistically, I then go on to explore a different, and empirical, approach to this issue in Section 3.

It is often taken for granted that if the theoretical virtues are indeed capable of contributing to a theory's epistemic standing, then underdetermination will cease to be a problem.[11] After all, if the virtues have epistemic power, empirical equivalence is no longer sufficient for epistemic equivalence and, once the virtues are in play, appealing to them can settle previously worrisome cases. But this defence simply assumes that underdetermination will disappear once our notion of epistemic equivalence is suitably expanded and that therefore virtue-appeals will single out one theory over its competitors. As I will show in this section, this conclusion is premature. Simply because there is more to epistemic equivalence than empirical equivalence does not preclude even widespread underdetermination; it just means that the original argument reappears in a somewhat different guise. And in order to assess whether or not the virtues are capable of adequately addressing the underdetermination argument, it's this new problem – a version of the argument that explicitly incorporates the virtues – that needs to be examined.[12]

This new problem has received relatively little attention (but see Tulodziecki 2012a and Ivanova 2014). Perhaps this is due to the fact that it's tempting to think that the virtue strategy will resolve most, or even all cases of underdetermination, based on the fact that it is obvious how it can take care of at least some cases. Yet, this is not so. The basic idea behind underdetermination was always that there are no epistemic grounds on which to choose scientific theories. There is thus nothing inherently tying underdetermination to empirical equivalence; it just so happens that empirical equivalence became the de facto dividing line in many contemporary discussions, largely because this lined up with epistemic distinctions at stake in the realism debate. As a result, most discussions of underdetermination simply end with arguments for the theoretical virtues, assuming that once we invoke these extra epistemic criteria, underdetermination will largely disappear. This, however, is doing only half the work.

---

[11] See, for example, Schindler: "[I]f theoretical virtues were epistemic, the threat posed by UTE [underdetermination] could be fended off" (2018: 31); also "if theoretical virtues were epistemic, belief in a theory on the basis of these virtues would be justifiable and thus rational" (2018: 31).

[12] I originally develop this new problem, as well as several of the points in this section, in Tulodziecki (2012a).

The second part is clarifying exactly how and where the virtues enter the underdetermination argument, understanding the extent to which they can or cannot resolve potential cases, and evaluating what the general prospects for their successfully doing so are.

In 2.2, I'll briefly review the debate about the theoretical virtues. In 2.3, I'll reformulate the underdetermination argument in a way that explicitly takes the theoretical virtues into account. Then, in 2.4 and 2.5, I explain what is required in order to establish this new kind of underdetermination. I end by assessing how serious a problem this poses for both realists and anti-realists (2.6) and by drawing some general lessons about the prospects of underdetermination arguments in general (2.7).

2.2 The Theoretical Virtues Debate

The debate about the theoretical virtues has a long heritage. Kuhn, for example, proposed that scientists appeal to several virtues when evaluating theories: non-ad hocness, fertility, simplicity, unification, and consistency (1977: 332). However, Kuhn did not regard these virtues as epistemic, since in Kuhn's framework, theories don't progress towards approximate truth (1962). Kuhn's point was instead to show that evaluating scientific theories was not a straightforward matter: different scientists might give different weight to features such as the aforementioned and even understand them in different ways entirely. But Kuhn's point doesn't apply just to scientists – philosophers have also debated how individual virtues ought to be understood. One of the most contested and widely examined is simplicity. Already discussed in the 1950s and 1960s as part of more general debates about logical positivism,[13] it has been debated ever since, with different philosophers understanding it in significantly different ways (Sober 1975). The same is true for fertility/fruitfulness (Haufe 2024) and explanatory power (Boyd 1991, Psillos 1999, Tulodziecki 2011). Regardless of how realists understand individual virtues and which subset of virtues makes it onto their respective lists, however, their general line is to understand the theoretical virtues as epistemic. Psillos, for example, states that "[w]e also need to take into account several theoretical virtues such as coherence with other established theories, consilience, completeness, unifying power, lack of ad hoc features and capacity to generate novel predictions" (1999: 171). Similarly, Churchland writes "that observational excellence or 'empirical adequacy' is only one epistemic virtue among others of equal or comparable importance" (1985: 35; the virtues that Churchland cites

---

[13] Frank, for example, claims that "[t]he actual advance of science has always been engineered by a criterion of economy and simplicity" (1957: 350f.).

later in the same paragraph are simplicity, coherence, and explanatory power). In contrast to this stands the anti-realist position that takes the theoretical virtues to be merely pragmatic. Van Fraassen, for example, is explicit that for him the virtues "provide reasons for using a theory, or contemplating it, whether or not we think it true, and cannot rationally guide our epistemic attitudes and decisions" (1980: 87).

The task for realists is therefore to establish a link between the theoretical virtues and (approximate) truth. Yet, despite the fact that realists frequently invoke the virtues, there have only been comparatively few discussions explicitly trying to establish this connection (but see McMullin 1982, Psillos 1999: 165ff., Tulodziecki 2014, 2021). A recent attempt is Schindler (2018), who endorses Kuhn's five original virtues but, unlike Kuhn, defends the view that the virtues are epistemic. Moreover, he tries to argue "that a 'very virtuous' theory – i.e., a theory that possesses all of the five standard virtues – is likely to be true" (2018: 211). Schindler's and other realists' goal is to show *that* our best theories instantiate the theoretical virtues. In contrast, one of my central arguments in this Element is that the role the virtues play is determined not just by *whether* scientific theories do or don't possess them, but also by the *extent* to which they do so as well as by the extent to which the virtues do work in promoting scientific goals. I further argue that even presupposing both that our best theories have the virtues and that the virtues are epistemic (both of which I endorse, although not in the standard realist sense), this does not help realists fend off the underdetermination argument (this section and Section 3).

2.3 The New Underdetermination Argument[14]

A new formulation of the underdetermination argument that takes the theoretical virtues into account looks like this: A pair of theories is underdetermined just in case (i) they are logically incompatible and empirically equivalent, (ii) tie with respect to the theoretical virtues, and (iii) there are no other epistemic criteria relevant to theory-choice favouring one over the other. If these three conditions are met, theories are epistemically equivalent and since we therefore have no epistemic reason for choosing one of the theories over the other, underdetermination obtains. This argument is quite similar to the classic argument presented in 1.1, with two notable differences. The first is that it contains a new clause specifically about theoretical virtues; the second is a modification of the 'epistemic constraint' clause (which becomes (iii) in the new version of

---

[14] This subsection as well as the two following it might be especially relevant to the debate about theoretical virtues in metaphysics. There, empirical equivalence is usually regarded as a given, and therefore it is often thought that "choosing theories on the basis of theoretical virtues is appropriate across the board" (Bueno & Shalkowski 2020: 459).

the argument) that seeks to specify what is and isn't a legitimate epistemic criterion for theory-choice. This clause replaces what was previously Premise 2. Whereas before, this ruled out anything besides the empirical evidence, it now leaves space for the virtues. As before, however, opponents of the underdetermination argument are likely to argue that even this view of theory-choice is too restrictive and that there are plenty of other criteria – besides the empirical evidence and the theoretical virtues – that play distinctly epistemic roles in theory-choice. To give just one example, it has been argued that one's theories need to pass methodological muster. Since the present focus is on theoretical virtues, I won't take up this issue here, but merely note in passing that it's straightforward enough to extend both the revised underdetermination argument and the arguments in this subsection to other potentially epistemic criteria (for a more detailed discussion of methodological criteria, see Tulodziecki 2013).

One further note on clause (ii): for the purposes of this argument and this section, I'll keep the category of theoretical virtues neutral with respect to its members. As I already suggested, there are many different kinds of virtues that come with different degrees of controversy. The argument of this section is indifferent with respect to how the virtue category is constituted and applies to whatever one's preferred subset of theoretical virtues is, whether this be Kuhn's original five virtues (Kuhn 1977: 332, also endorsed by Schindler 2018), or the looser list of virtues taken to be explanatory (such as those endorsed by Churchland 1985 or Psillos 1999).

As we already saw, anti-realists tend to deny the theoretical virtues any epistemic power. As we also noted, an underlying assumption shared by both realists and anti-realists is that *if* it could be shown that the virtues are epistemic, the underdetermination problem would be solved. It is for this reason that realists devote so much time to establishing the truth-conduciveness of the virtues and anti-realists their merely pragmatic role. For now, I want to shelve the discussion of whether the virtues are in fact epistemically potent and argue that, regardless of whether they are, showing that the virtues possess epistemic power is not enough to evade the underdetermination argument. Anti-realists can grant that the virtues – whichever subgroup is selected – are epistemic but maintain a new type of underdetermination that arises from problems with assessing epistemic equivalence. Ultimately, this will allow them to hold on to an argument that functions more or less analogously to the way the old argument functioned in the original debate about empirical equivalence. Thus, contrary to prevailing opinion, establishing that the virtues are epistemically significant is not enough to undercut underdetermination.

2.4 Comparing Theoretical Virtues

So, for the sake of argument, let's assume that we are faced with a number of theories fulfilling our three conditions. Now, understanding the difficulties with comparing the theoretical virtues turns on recognizing that theories can meet these conditions – and therefore be epistemically equivalent – in several different ways. We already noted that even assessing empirical equivalence is not always straightforward. Assessing epistemic equivalence adds an additional layer of complication, since it involves both empirical equivalence but also virtue equivalence. It therefore involves both balancing these two types of equivalence against each other as well as assessing equivalence within the two categories individually.

Assuming empirical equivalence, there are three main ways in which theories can be epistemically equivalent to each other with respect to the theoretical virtues: (a) they can exhibit the same virtues to the same degree, (b) they can exhibit the same virtues to different degrees, or (c) they can exhibit different virtues altogether (to whatever degrees). We can think of the first case, in which the theories exhibit the same virtues to the same degree, as exact epistemic equivalence. In this case, the two (or however many) theories have all the same virtues and do equally well with respect to all of them. This seems a generally unlikely scenario, since the odds of two different theories scoring equally strongly with respect to, say, explanatory power and generation of novel predictions and equally weakly with respect to, say, consilience or fruitfulness, are low. It's not impossible, however, and it might be exactly what we want to say about Earman's metaphysically unexciting cases, such as two Newtonian universes with absolute space, one at rest and the alternative universe one whose centre of gravity is moving with a particular constant velocity with respect to the centre of gravity of the world that is at rest with respect to absolute space. At any rate, it's clear that if this type of equivalence were to obtain, the virtues would fail to select one theory over the other. In the second case, the theories exhibit the same virtues – again, say, explanatory power, generation of novel predictions, consilience, and fruitfulness – but differ with respect to how strongly they each instantiate these different virtues. The first might score high on explanatory power and novel predictions and do much worse with respect to consilience and fruitfulness; for the second, the situation is reversed. Yet, their overall scores match and they each receive the same amount of epistemic push from their respective virtues, taken altogether. Thus, as before, they are epistemically equivalent with respect to the virtues, albeit not in the same way. A variation on this is the third case, in which theories differ on the virtues they exhibit. Here, epistemic equivalence could come about in a number of different ways. Two theories might simply instantiate different virtues entirely, without overlap (i.e., each has only virtues the other doesn't), or they might partially overlap (i.e., both instantiate some of the same virtues while differing on others). Lastly, one theory might exhibit a subset of the virtues of the other, such that all its virtues are shared with its competitor, but that competitor exhibits additional ones besides.

These are all the ways in which theories can be epistemically equivalent, but obviously this equivalence doesn't follow as a matter of course; there are also a number of ways in which it can fail. Take the case just discussed, for example, in which one theory's virtues are a proper subset of another's, and the latter therefore exhibits a greater number of virtues in total. Despite having more virtues overall, this does not mean that that theory is therefore automatically epistemically superior. It could be that both theories instantiate virtues that are valued highly and that the theory with fewer virtues does much better on those highly valued virtues than the one that has a greater total number. Further, if the virtues that it has in addition aren't valued very strongly, even a greater overall number will not be enough to make up for its deficiency in virtue-strength and it will therefore be epistemically inferior. For example, one might well prefer on epistemic grounds a theory that scores highly on unifying and explanatory power, novel predictions, and consilience to one that barely scores on these but instead exhibits relatively high degrees of simplicity or elegance.

Empirical equivalence adds a further complication since it's not necessary for epistemic equivalence. It might often take precedence over the other virtues, but there are also cases in which the theoretical virtues might trump evidence. Compare, for example, a theory that does slightly less well in terms of evidence than another but also exhibits a long list of important virtues, with a competitor that does slightly better in terms of evidence but does very badly with respect to any of the highly valued virtues. Even granting a theory's empirical components special privilege in general, it's easy enough to see how situations like these might violate such privilege. Similarly, a theory might not apply to a certain class of phenomena and therefore be silent on them, while another theory covers them. The first theory might thus apply to a much more limited domain, but still do extremely well in other ways. Its competitor, in contrast, might apply to the phenomena neglected by the first, thus exhibiting at least some degree of unifying power, but nevertheless be overall clunky, with its unification perhaps the result of highly contrived ad hoc modifications, while also showing little potential for novel predictions or avenues for further research. It might even have been generated via one of the more far-fetched Duhem-Quine strategies. In this case, even though the first theory covers fewer phenomena than the second, it would not be at all unreasonable for scientists to prefer it, and to do so on epistemic grounds. In neither of these cases do we have empirical equivalence and in both theoretical virtues trump evidence. We can further imagine similar predicaments in which one theory does slightly better in terms of evidence, the other slightly better in terms of virtues, and in which the two options are ultimately judged to be epistemically equivalent.

2.5 Assessing Theoretical Virtue Equivalence

However, for simplicity's sake, let's ignore empirical equivalence considerations for the moment and presuppose that empirical equivalence is required for epistemic equivalence. Incorporating the virtues into our epistemic assessment raises a number of questions: How should different virtues be weighed against each other? How do we determine to what extent a theory exhibits a particular virtue? How do we compare the same virtue in different theories? What kinds of factors matter in assessing the epistemic weight of a virtue in a theory? Does it depend just on the theory itself or other, external factors, such as what other theories are available, scientific or social context, what live scientific problems most urgently need solving, and so on? Can and/or should we rank the virtues? Without answers to at least some of these questions, it's hard to see how we could implement non-arbitrary comparisons among the virtues or among theories possessing them.

The main takeaway from these considerations is that in order to assess whether two theories are virtue-equivalent or not requires being able to compare the virtues. This in turn would seem to require, at a minimum, at least a partial ranking of the virtues, possibly under strongly heterogeneous conditions. Yet, it seems unrealistic to expect this to be forthcoming. A ranking would require some more precise way of establishing a hierarchy of virtues, perhaps by assigning numerical values, and it is hard to see how this would or could be anything other than arbitrary. But even if we had such a ranking, it would be insufficient for our purposes, since on its own it would not be enough to allow us to determine whether a greater number of low-ranking virtues ought to count as much as a lower number of high-ranking ones. The upshot is that, either way, to avoid an epistemic impasse, it's necessary to establish some non-arbitrary, epistemic basis for comparison of the different virtues. Without this, one cannot say whether two theories are virtue-equivalent, without which one cannot determine whether they are epistemically equivalent, without which one cannot determine whether they constitute a case of underdetermination or not.

Part of what makes developing a ranking of the virtues so difficult is that possessing theoretical virtues is usually not simply a matter of a theory having or not having those virtues, but instead a matter of degree. The relevant question is thus usually about the extent to which a virtue is exhibited, not whether it is exhibited in the first place. These already significant problems are compounded by the fact that many virtues are inherently comparative in nature and therefore how well a theory does with respect to them depends not just on the theory itself, but also on what other theories are available.[15] For instance, whether a theory coheres well with other existing theories depends on what those other theories are, what their epistemic status is, how well entrenched we take them to be, and so on. Take, for example, the 60-year-long twentieth-century debate between fixists and mobilists about whether or not the continents moved. According to fixists, continents and ocean basins were fixed in their positions, having been in the same place since the formation of the Earth. According to mobilists, continents slowly moved ("drifted") over geological time and into their current positions. As Frankel shows in his four-volume masterpiece on the history of continental drift (2012), much of the debate between these two camps turned on attitudes towards paleomagnetism, the study of the magnetization of rocks and sediments and of how these record the Earth's magnetic field during their periods of formation. Paleomagnetism provided geophysical evidence for mobilism, supporting the view that the continents had drifted. In fact, paleomagnetic findings made sense only on a view on which the continents had moved relative to each other, but most Earth scientists at the time were fixists and did not accord much importance to these findings: "[t]o some fixists, paleomagnetists seemed like magicians with their bag full of tricks. They were even derisively called paleomagicians, full of hocus pocus" (Frankel 2012, Vol 1: 16). Fixists instead argued that mobilism and some of its purported explanations were in conflict with seismology, the theory of glaciation, as well as with uniformitarianism, the principle that the geological processes shaping the Earth have operated at more or less the same rate throughout history. When Wegener (1915) proposed massive and relatively rapid movements of the continents, his critics accused him of reintroducing catastrophism, the idea that Earth's history is not uniform but punctuated by sudden and violent events. Fixists and mobilists thus debated not just the extent to which their different views cohered with other theories – mobilism cohered much better with paleomagnetism, fixism cohered better with several other geological theories – but also whether and to what extent this coherence mattered.[16] Both mobilism and

---

[15] For some attempts at taxonomizing the virtues, see McMullin (1996) and Keas (2018). Since the details of these taxonomies don't matter for my purposes, I won't discuss them further at this point.

[16] The history of this controversy is both complex and fascinating. For a quick overview, see Frankel 2012, Vol. 1: Chapter 1. For a deeper dive into paleomagnetic issues, see his 2012, Vol. 2.

fixism cohered with other existing theories, but on its own this coherence was neither here nor there.

Similarly for external consistency: If a theory in one domain is currently consistent with theories in another because theories in that other domain are woefully underdeveloped, one might assign less value to that theory's external consistency than if it was consistent with a theory in another domain that has been well-entrenched for a long time, is highly regarded, and for which it has been extremely difficult to find a consistent complement. Put another way, it would be an enormous achievement for a theory to be consistent with a theory in another domain when a central and important problem has been to find just such a theory, and after a history of failed attempts (the many and ongoing endeavours to square quantum mechanics and general relativity with each other are a good example of this). In contrast, it would be less of an achievement for a theory to be consistent with a theory in another domain when that domain is new and contains only theories that are presently underbaked. In this way, the 'same' virtue – external consistency with other theories – could (and should) be valued quite differently in different circumstances. We can imagine similar scenarios for other comparative virtues, such as being the best explanation.

Then there are virtues for which it is unclear whether they are comparative or not. Take fruitfulness, for example: some theories are obviously fruitful and some obviously fail to be fruitful, by anyone's standards. But what about the grey zone, populated by theories that are neither outstanding nor terrible, but the best of a number of mediocre options, all of which have significant problems? How are we to weigh their respective degrees of fruitfulness against each other, if at all? Or take the continental drift debate again: Fixism, while supported by observations of seemingly stable landmasses, struggled to explain the distribution of similar fossils and rock formations across different continents. Mobilism could explain this distribution, but lacked a plausible mechanism for continental movement. Fixism was much narrower in outlook than mobilism, discouraging other explanations for geological phenomena, but made headway on specialist puzzles and problems. Mobilism inspired many new questions in several different areas but could hardly answer any of them (at least until relatively late in the debate, see Frankel 2012, Vol. 3). How should these two very different types of fruitfulness be compared? Similarly, cases of simplicity or elegance might sometimes, but not always, be judged comparatively. Thus, even if we could solve some of the more 'straightforward' problems with respect to the theoretical virtues, such as unambiguously determining what should count as a theoretical virtue and whether a theory possesses it, we are still left with the two significant problems of how to quantify and/or numerically rank the virtues and how to compare different virtues against each other.

2.6 Upshot for Realists and Anti-realists

We can thus see that an underdetermination argument incorporating the virtues brings with it its own set of problems. But what is the upshot of this argument for realists and anti-realists? Earlier, we saw that it was important for anti-realists to establish that all scientific theories are underdetermined, because it is only this generalized version of the underdetermination argument that threatens scientific knowledge and, therefore, scientific realism. After all, realists don't deny that there could be genuine cases of underdetermination and that when or if those cases arise, one should suspend epistemic judgement. They just deny that those cases are widespread or even common. In fact, as the discussion about what counts as a genuine rival shows, they think those cases are exceedingly rare. The new version of the underdetermination argument thus seems a positive development for realists, since the added complexity resulting from incorporating the virtues lessens the anti-realists' chances of producing the kind of argument they require: a general and in-principle argument indiscriminately targeting all scientific theories. In the old argument, anti-realists tried to fulfil this generality condition by seeking to establish a version of the EET that would apply to any theory whatsoever, and by denying that there are criteria besides the evidence that play an epistemic role in theory-choice. Once the more elaborate theoretical virtue version of the argument is in play, they now need, in addition, to provide a general argument establishing virtue-equivalence. The new underdetermination argument therefore helps the realist in two ways: first, by winnowing down the number of potential cases of underdetermination, through imposing extra constraints on what counts as an epistemically equivalent rival; second, by making it more difficult for anti-realists to produce the guarantee of underdetermination they require in order for their argument to have the serious epistemic consequences they ascribe to it.

What avenues are open to the anti-realist given this new predicament? What sort of generalist argument for virtue-equivalence might be in the offing? Earlier, we saw two different strategies with respect to establishing empirical equivalence: the first involved modifying competitors by making adjustments necessary for achieving empirical equivalence, and doing so repeatedly if called for. The second was to provide sceptical hypotheses or algorithms to generate empirically equivalent competitors in one fell swoop. These same strategies are open to anti-realists in the theoretical virtue case: they need to provide either a way to make adjustments in a way that can guarantee virtue-equivalence via an updated Duhem-Quine manoeuvre, or else find a way to generate wholesale virtue-equivalent rivals. But as the aforementioned complications have made clear, it's much harder to demonstrate epistemic than empirical equivalence.

And although it seemed as if these complications worked in favour of the realist, it turns out that anti-realists can turn these very same complications to their own advantage. Just as anti-realists cannot generate an in-principle argument for epistemic equivalence, realists will have trouble demonstrating the epistemic superiority of one theory over another in a way that doesn't presuppose the very point they are trying to establish. After all, if we don't know how to assess and compare the virtues, how exactly can we determine that one theory is epistemically superior to another on that basis?

Also, anti-realists need only show, for every theory, that it has at least one rival. Given that, as we already saw, the situation is not simply one of counting up the 'haves' vs. the 'have-nots' and that different theories might instantiate different virtues, it seems overwhelmingly likely that anti-realists will always be in a position to propose a rival that instantiates at least some virtues, thereby opening the proverbial can of worms. Note that even obviously unscientific rivals are likely to exhibit at least some virtues. At the extreme end, one might get them to do so in a way that mirrors the artificial constructions we saw in the case of empirical equivalence. After all, "everything is caused by fairies" certainly exhibits some degree of simplicity and unifying power. Similarly, numerology, in purporting to uncover hidden meaning and patterns through a single numerical framework, doesn't just have unifying power, but great scope in applying to individuals, businesses, institutions, and even whole societies. Now, we might well want to exclude such 'theories' on other grounds, but the point is precisely that plenty of theories have virtues and so it's not on the basis of theoretical virtues alone that their epistemic status is determined, as the initial realist response would have it. If need be, anti-realists can introduce virtues into otherwise less promising candidates artificially, through brute force mental engineering, using strategies similar to those they used to achieve some of the more questionable cases of empirical equivalence. Someone might object that more evidence will eventually select scientific over fairy theories and that therefore this kind of underdetermination is only transient, but we also already saw that the adjustment strategy can be repeated, effectively rendering such cases permanently transient.

Questionable as this approach may be, it raises some new – legitimate – questions associated with the virtues, if they are to fulfil their intended role as tie-breakers in response to the original underdetermination argument, or at least with respect to the way that role is articulated in many realist responses. Given that certain virtues – say unifying power or simplicity – can be engineered into theories, does this 'cheapen' these virtues or is it merely an indicator that they were never truly epistemic in the first place? After all, if unifying power truly has epistemic power, it should have that power regardless of what theory it applies to. As a result, even "everything is caused by fairies" should carry at least some amount of epistemic weight in virtue of its unifying ability. One response is to bite the bullet and admit that adding unifying power to theories – even if unification by fairies – does, in fact, raise the epistemic standard of the theories it applies to. Still, one might argue, adding this kind of unification doesn't raise the theory's epistemic value enough to be significant, either because the overall epistemic value of this 'theory' is only minimal for other reasons, or because the virtue itself isn't powerful enough. This preserves the epistemic weight of the virtues instantiated in this way, but it also highlights again the importance of having a ranking or, more generally, a basis for being able to compare different virtues with each other in different instances. The second explicitly requires a way to judge the virtues against each other; the first requires a way to judge a theory's epistemic weight independently of either this virtue or the virtues altogether.

These difficulties for the realist now open up another possible position for the anti-realist: maintain that establishing virtue-equivalence is so complex that it's simply impossible to put the virtues to work in a principled epistemic way and that, therefore, we are fated to remain at an epistemic impasse. This impasse, in turn, will lead to a new kind of epistemic underdetermination, albeit different from the one we had in mind initially. The anti-realist no longer needs to show that there is epistemic equivalence among theories; instead, it is enough to show that theory-choice on the basis of the theoretical virtues is impossible. The underlying reason here does not matter, and it doesn't require any particular attitude towards the virtues, even denying that they are epistemic. All it requires is that the virtue situation be too epistemically messy to guarantee that we can make epistemically grounded choices whenever we need to.

Thus, we still have underdetermination, but not because there *are* no epistemic reasons, but because those reasons are simply too complex for us to get a systematic handle on, thereby making it impossible to put them to work in a way that disables the theoretical virtue version of the argument. The result is underdetermination by epistemic impasse. The upshot, however, is just the same as that of the old argument: we cannot choose scientific theories for epistemic reasons, threatening the possibility of scientific knowledge.

One obvious realist rejoinder is to argue that epistemic complexity is not related to how easily we are able to make the relevant judgements. After all, there are many complex situations in which we might be unable to articulate the reasons for our choices, yet in which the choices are easy. We routinely avoid certain kinds of accidents, adopt particular dialects or accents, add certain spices to elaborate meals, and so on. Why not think that choosing scientific theories also falls into this category? The reason this line of defence won't help the realist is that what's required to defuse the new underdetermination argument is not a demonstration that sometimes choices can be made even when all competitors have virtues (they can, and sometimes perhaps even on obviously epistemic grounds), but an argument that demonstrates that such choices can be made in principled and systematic ways in cases the anti-realist puts forward and that the realist wishes to dispute.

Remember here that the issue is not judging *whether* theories have virtues, but an epistemically grounded comparative assessment of theories all of which have some virtues. Importantly, this assessment needs to be the result of a process in which *the theoretical virtues themselves settle the epistemic question*. This last point is crucial. Realists might still want to dismiss sceptical hypotheses on other grounds, for example because they are not sufficiently scientific. This might well be a fine and good thing to do, but such a choice would not be based on the theoretical virtues (or the empirical evidence) and therefore amount to a choice violating the constraints of the new underdetermination argument.

Thus, once faced with two theories both of which exhibit at least some virtues, for those virtues to settle debates about underdetermination or theory-choice, we need to have a more substantial account either of how the virtues work or how to compare them. After all, the point of the new argument is not to show that we can't choose on epistemic grounds or that there is no underdetermination, but instead to demonstrate that simply appealing to the virtues doesn't settle the matter, a central presupposition of the vast majority of underdetermination discussions in the realism debate.

To argue that sometimes we can resolve cases despite their complexity is therefore no solution to the new underdetermination problem. Instead, realists need to disable the anti-realist position that we can always come up with rivals that produce sufficient messiness to make epistemic choices in non-arbitrary ways impossible. And anti-realists can capitalize on this new epistemic messiness to come up with just the kind of rival they need, in the same way in which they used sceptical hypotheses and algorithms to do this job with respect to empirical equivalence. Indeed, and counterintuitively, one might view the theoretical virtues as fulfilling a role similar to that of algorithms and sceptical hypotheses before: to provide anti-realists with ways to generate rivals that incapacitate the realist's epistemic choices.

2.7 Conclusion

The complexity involved in assessing the virtues means that virtue-equivalence doesn't seem to favour either realists or anti-realists. While the idea that they are epistemic features besides the evidence initially seemed to give an edge to realists, the fact that assessing them was nigh impossible brings the anti-realist back into the picture. The upshot with respect to the theoretical virtues is that, epistemic or not, they are incapable of guiding theory-choice. Note one important difference to the original scenario, however: it is an open question at this point whether different virtues are truly incommensurable and therefore situations relying on their epistemic complexity can genuinely not be resolved, or whether this is simply an extremely hard thing to do.

Further, the aforementioned line of argument suggests that in order for virtue-considerations to do any work, they need to be tied more closely to actual scientific theories as well as actual scientific practice. Abstract underdetermination arguments that kick the ball back and forth between realists and anti-realists don't settle the matter either way. What's worse, they seem to be mostly an academic exercise quite besides the point of sincere and good-faith attempts geared towards understanding what sorts of criteria have genuine influence on the epistemic standing of our scientific theories. In the same way in which the original underdetermination argument sparked abstract debates involving algorithms and sceptical hypotheses – not live options in the lab (notwithstanding the possibility of being a brain in a vat) – the new argument sparks debates about utopian and unrealistic measures of the virtues and their ad hoc incorporation into potential rivals in ways that are not reflective of actual scientific practice. Moreover, if the virtues are indeed epistemic, their epistemic power *should* extend to all kinds of theories: genuinely scientific ones, genuine rivals, borderline cases, as well as philosophical ad hoc scenarios generated merely for the sake of argument.

The lesson here is that the potentially epistemic impact of the virtues, if any, comes not from simply 'being had' by a theory or not, and not even from being exhibited to varying degrees, but from how exactly those virtues are put to work in live scientific predicaments and contexts. It is for this reason that it's important to study the virtues on the ground, in their 'live habitat', because only this can tell us why they have held such systematic appeal for scientists themselves, and not just for philosophers.

3 The Epistemic Labour View of Theoretical Virtues

3.1 Introduction

One of the points of Section 2 is that when assessing scientific theories with respect to the theoretical virtues, this assessment is not simply a matter of having vs. not having the virtues, since many virtues are inherently comparative and/or come in degrees. The situation is, in fact, much more complicated than this since the epistemic power of a theory's virtues – and even whether a theory instantiates a particular virtue – can also change over time. In some sense, this is an obvious consequence of the fact that some virtues are comparative: if their potential depends on what other theories are available – say when talking about external consistency – then it's clear that a theory can start out by being consistent with the dominant theory in a highly relevant, adjacent field, but later become inconsistent with such a theory, purely in virtue of the fact that the other theory changed, but nothing at all changed with respect to the theory under consideration itself.

Even virtues that don't seem inherently comparative can be instantiated to different degrees, in the very same theory, over time. Take explanatory power, for example: one might think a theory either explains the phenomena well or it doesn't, but of course even that depends on what other explanations are available. And we don't even need to invoke "best" explanations in order to make the point. It's entirely plausible that at some earlier time a theory's explanation is good (maybe it's insightful and also the only one) but that at some later time it's looking merely mediocre (perhaps other theories now also explain the phenomena, some in more depth, or because there are now more phenomena standing in need of an explanation). The same can be said for nearly every virtue on the list and in this way even non-inherently or non-obviously comparative virtues depend on what else is available. I might think my dog is well-trained, but it matters whether we're talking about my local neighbourhood or the Westminster agility championship.

These are just some of the reasons why it's a mistake to focus solely on a theory and its virtues in isolation – theories are not static 'objects' but situated and evolving theoretical clusters, constantly in flux. This reinforces the conclusion of Section 2 that no general, in-principle argument addressing a new version of the underdetermination argument that incorporates the theoretical virtues is possible. That, and the nature of the problems with that general argument suggests that *if* the virtues can be put to work in underdetermination contexts, it will be on a case-by-case basis. This section develops this view in more detail. Attitudes about the theoretical virtues tend to align with the two main positions in the scientific realism debate – realism and anti-realism – but, as we will see, this is not a matter of necessity. In this section, I make the case for separating these debates from each other, in the process carving out a new role for the theoretical virtues that is neither realist nor anti-realist. Specifically, I will develop what I call the 'Epistemic Labour View of Theoretical Virtues'. On this view, there is no inherent connection between the virtues and truth, yet the virtues are capable of playing an epistemic role. They do so exactly when they work to promote one of the many genuinely epistemic goals of science. Thus, contra the realist, the theoretical

Underdetermination and Theoretical Virtues

virtues are not truth-conducive but also, contra the anti-realist, they are not merely pragmatic. I first lay out (3.2) the underlying motivation for the Epistemic Labour View, followed by a discussion of pluralism about epistemic goals (3.3), and discussions of what it means for the virtues to do epistemic work (3.4) and for them to be epistemically inert (3.5).

3.2 Severing Epistemicity from Truth

As we saw, the epistemic/pragmatic distinction with respect to the virtues is usually mapped onto the epistemic divisions among realists and anti-realists. Underlying this mapping is the debate's dichotomy between two epistemic aims of science: (approximate) truth for the realist and empirical adequacy for the anti-realist. Both parties agree that theoretical virtues are epistemic if they contribute to their respective aims; it's just that they differ on what those aims are and therefore on what can legitimately be said to contribute to them. Since for the anti-realist the epistemic aim is empirical adequacy, the only virtues(s) that can make epistemic contributions are related to empirical evidence. All other virtues (with the possible exception of internal consistency) are non-epistemic or pragmatic, which in this case, as the ECT makes clear, are synonymous. Because realists have as their goal (approximate) truth, they can in principle allow for a wider category of epistemic virtues, including theoretical virtues not directly related to empirical evidence. In the anti-realists' case, it's largely clear how accounting for empirical evidence contributes to the larger epistemic aim of empirical adequacy (but see Section 2), but there is no such obvious connection between other theoretical virtues and (approximate) truth. For realists, theoretical virtues are epistemic if they are truth-conducive and therefore establishing the truth-conduciveness of the virtues is their way of establishing that there really are factors besides the empirical evidence that make epistemic contributions to our scientific theories.[17] In short, it is for reasons related to realist and anti-realist attitudes about the aim of science that the theoretical virtue debate takes the form it does.

However, these two positions are not the only possible ones to take with respect to the virtues. As this section will show, thinking through how the virtues are used in actual, live scenarios is suggestive of a third option that severs the link between the virtues' epistemicity and theories' (approximate)

---

[17] I should note here that this is so for the 'classic realisms' (of, e.g., Boyd and Psillos) and their variations (structural realism, entity realism, semi-realism, etc.). My position on the virtues seems to me quite compatible with, and perhaps even welcome by, some of the more recent realisms, such as Chang's 'Realism for Realistic People' (2022) and Massimi's 'Perspectival Realism' (2022); see also Subsection 3.3.

truth. Once we reject the dichotomy of empirical adequacy and (approximate) truth as the only two goals of science, we also open up a new position for the theoretical virtues, namely that they can be epistemic without contributing to either of these goals and in particular without being truth-conducive. Thus, showing that the theoretical virtues play an epistemic role does not have to amount to linking them to truth; they can do so through contributing to other epistemic aims. As a result, once we expand our notion of what counts as an epistemic goal of science, it is perfectly consistent to admit that it might well be the case that we are often not licensed to infer a theory's (approximate) truth. But, we are not thereby committed to the anti-realist view that, therefore, empirical evidence is the *only* epistemically relevant factor in theory-choice. And, contra the realist, even if there were *no* theoretical virtues that are truth-conducive, this does not mean that there could not be plenty of epistemically relevant factors that make significant epistemic contributions to the various other epistemic goals of science. Driven by these considerations, the Epistemic Labour View of Theoretical Virtues reconceives the traditional realist understanding of 'epistemic' and embraces a pluralist view about what counts as a genuinely epistemic goal of science, carving out an epistemic role for the virtues that is independent of any connection they might have to truth. Further, unlike on existing views, it's not the mere possession of the virtues that has epistemic consequences; instead, the virtues function epistemically only when they do work in promoting live scientific aims.

3.3 Pluralism about Epistemic Goals

What does the Epistemic Labour View of Virtues look like in more detail? Let's start by getting clearer on the meaning of 'epistemic'. On the usual, realist reading, the virtues are regarded as epistemic exactly when they are truth-conducive. Steel, for example, notes "that the characteristic feature of epistemic values is that they promote, either intrinsically or extrinsically, the attainment of truths" (2010: 32). McMullin already puts it this way in 1982, noting that "[s]uch characteristic values [the theoretical virtues] I will call epistemic, because they are presumed to promote the truth-like character of science" (18). By saying that the virtues are truth-conducive, realists mean that a theory that has the virtues is more likely to be true than false and, in fact, likely to be at least approximately true. Schindler, for example, makes this thought explicit relatively recently, writing that his "central argument for realism is that a very virtuous theory – i.e., a theory possessing all of the standard virtues – is likely to be true" (2018: 2). It is because of this that realists think the theoretical virtues can help with making epistemic choices about which theories to prefer, including tie-breaking choices in cases of underdetermination: the virtues are taken to be *signs* of truth (and, in particular, signs of truths about unobservables), and one should therefore prefer theories that have the virtues over those that don't. Since, as we already saw, for realists the ultimate epistemic goal of science is truth, the virtues are epistemic in virtue of contributing to that goal and therefore *because* they are truth-conducive. This view doesn't rule out other goals for science (non-epistemic ones, or ones subsidiary to truth), but it does mean that a requirement for something being epistemic is that it directly or indirectly contribute to achieving the realists' ultimate epistemic aim. It is also for this reason that it has been so important for realists to establish the connection between the theoretical virtues and (approximate) truth: if this connection is in doubt, so is (for realists) the epistemic status and value of the virtues.

In contrast, the Epistemic Labour View expands the notion of what counts as epistemic by embracing pluralism about the epistemic goals of science. Once we do so, we open up the possibility of the virtues being epistemic in ways other than their being truth-conducive. As before, it's still the case that a virtue counts as epistemic just in case it contributes to the epistemic goals of science; it's just that now, instead of one epistemic goal, there are many. Therefore, instead of a virtue's epistemic status being limited to its being conducive to truth specifically, this status is now expanded to its ability to contribute to achieving any one of the many epistemic goals of science. On the Epistemic Labour View, a virtue is epistemic just in case it is epistemic-goal-promoting.

The realist's epistemic goal monism is truth-centric: truth is the ultimate, most important, and only genuinely epistemic goal. According to epistemic goal pluralism, there are many different genuinely epistemic goals in their own right, with truth just being one of these. On the monist view, other epistemic goals are subservient to the overriding goal of truth; they are means to an end, truth is that end, and they are epistemically valuable only to the extent to which they contribute to that end. On the pluralist view, different epistemic goals are independent; they are not means towards some other, more fundamental end, and they do not derive their epistemic value from standing in a special relation to truth or, indeed, anything else. On the monist view, epistemic activities are geared towards truth-seeking, where pluralism allows for a wide range of epistemic activities and pursuits, viewing these as equally epistemically legitimate endeavours. According to the monist, an activity or theoretical virtue counts as epistemic just in case it is truth-conducive. According to the pluralist, an activity or virtue counts as epistemic as long as it contributes to achieving any epistemic goal, even (or perhaps especially) when this goal is independent of truth.[18]

What other kinds of epistemic goals are there? Here are some possibilities, in no particular order, some larger, some smaller: non-realist notions of truth, non-traditional notions of knowledge and justification, understanding, reliability, generating solutions to puzzles and problems of various sizes, managing the world (Bhakthavatsalam & Cartwright 2017), avoiding error, difficulty-free solutions (Frankel 2012, Vol. 1), identifying causal relations, unifying different phenomena or different domains, explanations, accurate representations, models, laws, idealizations, analytical tools, producing scientific phenomena, describing phenomena, subsuming phenomena under laws, establishing and ordering domains, mathematizing a domain, integrating different research programmes (whether methodologically or in terms of subject matter), developing new instruments, living up to certain scientific standards (upholding good experimental protocols, performing rigorous hypothesis-testing, making sure instruments are well-calibrated, etc.), and, lastly, some of the myriad highly concrete and specific goals making up everyday scientific life.

The idea that science has many and diverse goals is, of course, not new. Neither is the idea that truth is not the only or even predominant aim of science. Kitcher, for example, has assailed the traditional notion of the pursuit of truth as part of the "myth of purity" (2001: Chapter 7). Kellert et al. (2006) make clear that one "implication of our pluralist outlook is that scientific approaches and theories should not be evaluated against the ideal of providing the single complete and comprehensive truth about a domain" (xxiv), and more recently Cartwright et al. (2022) take issue with the assumption "that the general aim of science is objective knowledge, or truth" (18).[19] One might question whether aims like the aforementioned are adequate candidates for being genuinely epistemic but here, too, there is excellent precedent. One particularly popular option that has emerged in recent years as an epistemic replacement for truth is

---

[18] An intermediate position combining features of both goal monism and goal pluralism is alethic pluralism, which involves holding that truth is the only epistemic goal, but also being a pluralist about truth itself. In addition to being an epistemic goal pluralist, I am also an alethic pluralist, but the latter is not an essential component of the Epistemic Labour View.

[19] Interestingly, when pluralism about aims is tied to discussions of scientific success, this is done mostly in the context of empirical success, not epistemic success more generally (see, for example, Chang 2018). It is also worth stressing explicitly that even though pluralism is not unpopular, debates about the theoretical virtues and underdetermination in the context of the realism debate still very much rely on the dichotomy between truth and empirical adequacy.

understanding.[20] In particular, there are substantive non-factivist views articulating understanding in ways that don't require true belief but that also explicitly argue that "understanding is a candidate for the purely epistemic aim of science" (Potochnik 2015: 75). On Potochnik's view, for example, understanding is a much better candidate for science's epistemic aim than truth, since it can accommodate false but routinely used and even essential parts of science, such as idealizations.[21] It has also been argued that such views allow false theories to produce genuine understanding (de Regt & Gijsbers 2016). Another recent candidate is reliability, proposed by Cartwright et al. (2022), and also articulated and defended as an epistemic aim. Yet another avenue is opened up by the recent pragmatist trends to revitalize a number of fundamental concepts, including 'truth', 'knowledge', and 'reality'. Kitcher, for example, embraces a melding of traditional correspondence and pragmatist theories of truth (2012: Chapter 5), and Chang proposes to reframe both truth and knowledge in terms of operational coherence, which "consists in aim-oriented coordination" (2022: 4). Like others, Chang is explicit that "we should break away from the view of scientific progress that is found at the foundation of standard scientific realism, which sees progress as an approach to the Truth" (2022: 213). Similarly, it is possible to break away from traditional conceptions of knowledge and justification. Philosophers of science have long emphasized the contextual nature, social dimensions, and situatedness of knowledge, as well as the idea – anathema to traditional accounts of knowledge from analytic epistemology – that it "can be appropriate to speak of knowledge even when there are ways of knowing a phenomenon that cannot be simultaneously embraced" (Longino 2004: 136). Massimi, in her work on perspectivism, understands scientific knowledge as having essential historical and cultural components (2022), and Chang (2022) has further developed his earlier accounts of knowledge as activity-based. With respect to justification, Longino advocates – again anathema to traditional accounts from analytic epistemology – "treating justification not just as a matter of relations between sentences, statements, or the beliefs and perceptions of an individual, but as a matter of relationships within and between communities of inquirers" (2004: 133–134). In a similar vein, Stegenga notes that "[s]cientific justification is special: it is communal and inter-subjective" (2024). All these approaches

---

[20] See, for example, Potochnik: "science does not aim to provide truth, but instead to provide understanding" (2015: 72).

[21] Potochnik sidesteps the question of whether there is one epistemic goal or many, since "nothing is at stake for [her] in that judgment" (2015: 75).

involve replacing the aim of science with something other than the traditional realist notion of truth, while also proposing options that are clearly epistemic.

What about the less grand aims of science further down the list, such as developing analytical tools, producing scientific phenomena, identifying causal relations, or unifying different domains? Should we regard these as epistemic goals in their own right or as merely subsidiary to something further up the epistemic flagpole? While my view is that many of these are indeed genuinely epistemic in their own right, I won't argue for this here, since this is not an essential component of the Epistemic Labour View of Virtues. That's because, as we just saw, there are already enough genuinely epistemic competitors to realist-truth for an interesting and substantive pluralism about epistemic goals that can sustain the view of the virtues presented here: that the theoretical virtues are not truth-conducive in the traditional sense but play an epistemic role as long as they promote any of the epistemic goals of science. My own understanding of this pluralism is liberal, embracing as one of its components genuine alethic pluralism (i.e., pluralism about different, competing notions of truth itself), as well as the idea that both abstract and concrete epistemic goals of science are not static, but change and evolve (for example, through Chang's epistemic iterations). However, neither is necessary for the Epistemic Labour View; neither is being able to draw a sharp distinction between 'epistemic' and 'non-epistemic' or 'wholly/purely epistemic' and 'partially epistemic', nor the idea that if a goal is epistemic, it thereby doesn't also fall into some other category (practical, social, instrumental, etc.). It's irrelevant to the core of this view whether less ambitious aims are epistemic in their own right or merely subsidiary to something else, as long as that something else is not, in every instance, the realist notion of truth. The virtues can thus support an epistemic goal directly or via a detour of smaller goals; either way, it's possible for the virtues to take on a genuinely epistemic function – doing work in promoting the various epistemic aims of science, without being truth-conducive in the realist sense.[22] Note that, of course, it's still possible for the virtues to promote realist-truth (indeed, it is one way for them to play an epistemic role), but doing so in specific instances is

---

[22] It's worth mentioning here that, if instead of embracing epistemic goal pluralism, one merely replaces traditional realist-truth with an alternative notion, this opens up a new way to argue that the virtues are truth-conducive after all: just because there are good counterexamples to the view that there is a systematic and inherent connection between the virtues and traditional realist truth doesn't mean these would be similarly effective for the various replacement notions. Even if it's false that the virtues are conducive to realist-truth, this does not mean that they're not conducive to other kinds of truth. This would obviously be incompatible with the traditional varieties of selective realism, but perhaps be a realistic (!) option for 'realism for realistic people', that is, for Chang's truth-as-operational-coherence (2022).

very different from their being truth-*conducive*. The latter requires a systematic connection between the virtues and truth that can't be sustained. Being truth-promoting in particular cases is much weaker, since it requires no general or even special connection between the promoter and its relevant goal. For a virtue to promote a goal is therefore very different from its being a general sign that a goal has been met or that one is close to it.

How do scientists know whether epistemic goals are being met? Here, I follow Chang (2022), who "takes science (and inquiry in general) as something that people do, consisting of epistemic activities with various aims whose achievement we can actually assess (unlike absolute truth)" (4).[23] We might not always be in a position to judge whether our loftier goals, including different kinds of truths and knowledge, have been achieved, but we often do know whether our concrete aims have been met or to what extent we have made progress with respect to them. Some goals, such as Frankel's 'difficulty-free solutions', even have accessibility of judgement baked into their very name. Sometimes scientists have in mind clear and concrete goals, sometimes they are working towards larger goals of inquiry in less direct ways, sometimes their achievements are serendipitous, but either way, they routinely judge whether they have engaged in an epistemic accomplishment, regardless of whether this ultimately furthers a higher-level goal, such as truth, down the line. Moreover, this type of epistemic success is something that members of the relevant scientific communities are able to assess in real time, not something that others are able to judge only in hindsight, possibly decades or centuries later.

3.4 Epistemic Labour

I already mentioned that a central part of the Epistemic Labour View of Theoretical Virtues is its eponymous idea that the virtues function epistemically only when they do epistemic work, by which is meant that they promote scientifically live epistemic goals. How do the theoretical virtues do this? One of the best ways to see this is via detailed studies of scientific debates. In line with my earlier example, and due to the fact that it is one of the most comprehensive and remarkable such studies ever produced, I will focus on Frankel's work on continental drift (2012). Frankel's analysis shows – repeatedly and systematically – that different participants in the fixism/mobilism debate valued various virtues for their ability to promote their respective epistemic goals. It is impossible to do justice to even a small part of Frankel's almost 3,000 pages, but

---

[23] See also Stegenga (2023), who follows Laudan (1977) in speaking up for the importance of epistemic accessibility in judging whether scientific progress has been made.

some snippets should be sufficient to highlight the main point about the virtues I want to make.[24]

When Wegener published his continental drift theory in 1915, central scientific concerns included how mountains and other geological features were formed, the distribution of fossils as well as similarities in rock formation and other geological structures across continents, paleoclimatic data, and evidence of past glaciations. Wegener proposed that the continents were once joined together in a single supercontinent ("Pangaea") and that they then gradually drifted apart over millions of years, into their current positions. Wegener's theory was much broader and more general than existing theories, aiming to explain a wide range of geological and geophysical phenomena on a global scale. It was also highly interdisciplinary, seeking to integrate evidence from many different scientific disciplines into a single comprehensive framework. His predominant competitors were much less ambitious and instead of focusing on global patterns in geology and paleontology, they tended to focus on evidence from particular disciplines instead of pursuing different lines from multiple fields.

In 2.5, we already saw that both mobilists and fixists valued coherence with other theories, but that mobilists emphasized coherence with paleomagnetism whereas fixists placed greater importance on coherence with other widely accepted geological theories, such as the theory of glaciation, uniformitarianism, and principles from seismology. But this is not the only virtue that played an epistemic role. For example, Frankel highlights that all participants in this debate – no matter their view – faced a large number of problems and puzzles and that, for all groups, pursuing difficulty-free solutions to these problems was a major epistemic goal.[25] While, on a general level, "in different contexts, consiliences ... were a recurrent theme through the mobilism debate" (2012: xvi), he specifically argues that mobilists placed great importance on "establish-[ing] consilience between different sets of results, and their efforts were especially important in improving the effectiveness of solutions" (2012: 19). Wegener in particular "was especially concerned to establish consilience between the marginal congruencies and geological similarities on either side of the Atlantic" (2012: 19). Frankel further shows that the paleomagnetic defence of continental drift, based on showing that the Earth's magnetic field is recorded in rocks during their formation, relied on "the consilience between the former latitudes of continents determined paleomagnetically and those inferred from paleoclimatic evidence" (2012: 21), "that the consilience between

---

[24] For further detail and better understanding, I highly recommend the whole four-volume set.
[25] For an overview of some of those problems, see 2012, Vol. 1: Chapter 1.

the paleontologic/paleoclimatic and paleomagnetic data strengthened support for mobilism" (2012, Vol. 2: 7), and that the "general consilience among the paleomagnetic, glacial, and paleobotanical data" (2012, Vol. 3: 360) played an important role for mobilists. Even though "there really were no competing fixist solutions for the paleomagnetic results that also explained this remarkable consilience" (2012, Vol 1: 30), "any consilience among Wegener's solutions carried little weight [among fixists] because each solution had its own, what they regarded as, fatal difficulties" (2012, Vol. 1: 87). Thus, in line with their respective epistemic foci, consilience was valued to a much greater extent by mobilists than fixists.

Similarly, mobilists and fixists differed on the importance they accorded to scope. As Frankel stresses, one of biggest issues "involved a clash between data from divergent sciences, viz., the geophysical and biological, rather than data from the same science" (1976: 306). As before, the fact that specialists and generalists in the debate were concerned with different scientific goals resulted in different virtues playing different epistemic roles for each side. Unsurprisingly, generalists valued broad scope more than specialists. This was once again especially so for Wegener, whose hypothesis "connected a large number of seemingly unrelated facts" (305) and synthesized "a vast abundance of different sorts of data" (305). Generalists – pursuing a broad geological theory – praised "the great range of Wegener's theory over so many seemingly diverse fields" (305) and were impressed with the ability of Wegener's theory "to connect seemingly unconnected events into coherent patterns" (306). Since specialists were predominantly concerned with problems in their own subfields, they accorded scope much less importance than the generalists and Frankel has argued that the "unfavorable reception [of Wegener's hypothesis] by the practicing earth scientists" was due at least in part to "their failure to appreciate its larger scope because of narrow specialization" (306). In his words, the "greater synthesizing ability of Wegener's theory was lost on the paleontologists and biologists ... the specialist overconcerned with details could not appreciate the overall scope of Wegener's theory" (318). Similarly, "[t]he corroborating facts were so diverse that their great variety was not appreciated by the specialists working in only their restricted field" (305), with specialists holding "fast to either the permanentist or contractionist viewpoint, despite the fact that neither had the overall scope of Wegener's hypothesis" (319).

What did the specialists value? Pursuing much narrower aims than Wegener and much more concerned with specific problems in individual disciplines, they faulted Wegener's account for its lack of ability to provide sufficiently detailed solutions and explanations in the much more local contexts they so highly valued (see 306). As a result, "[m]uch of the evidence Wegener had cited in favour of his theory was questioned by specialists from different research fields" (1978: 133), and "[r]epresentatives from the fields of paleogeography, entomology and botany all concluded that the data from their respective area did not support Wegener's theory" (132). The situation was complicated by the fact that there were differences in opinion as to what constituted the data most in need of explanation. Contractionists, who believed that the Earth was actively shrinking, were focused on the strength of biological data concerning the distribution of life forms, arguing that similarities in fossil assemblages on different continents could be explained by past land bridges that had since sunk or eroded away. According to them, the Earth's cooling and contraction was supposed to provide a mechanism for the existence and disappearance of these bridges. Permanentists, who believed in a fixed and unchanging Earth, privileged geophysical data supporting the principle of isostasy, according to which the Earth's crust floats on the denser mantle, similar to how icebergs float on water. They then used this principle to argue for the permanent positions of the continents and seafloors and against land bridges, which, they thought, would disturb the isostatic balance of the Earth's crust. For both, biological and geophysical data were in conflict, and while Wegener's theory could account for both, contractionists and permanentists both criticized Wegener's theory for its lack of specialist explanatory power, devaluing its (more superficial) explanatory diversity. Moreover, many specialists were confident that their own research programmes would prove sufficiently fertile to eventually conquer the difficulties in explaining the problematic data. They also made much of Wegener's biggest explanatory lacuna: a plausible mechanism for Drift.

Of course, this worry was also pressing for mobilists. In 1928, for example, Arthur Holmes attempted to give "a badly needed account of the forces responsible for continental drift" (Frankel 1978: Abstract). Holmes explicitly tried to address the question of how the continents could have moved across the sea floor and proposed 'seafloor thinning', a solution involving both convection currents and radioactivity. This solution was ultimately discarded, yet it illustrates the importance Drift advocates accorded to explanatory power in addressing the issue of identifying a plausible mechanism for Drift. Importantly, Holmes did not just provide one of the first attempts to provide a candidate for a drift mechanism, he also took care to spell out how his hypotheses could account for various non-Drift consequences. As Frankel puts it: "If the only consequence of Holmes' hypothesis had been its solving of Drift's 'engineering problem', and explanation of phenomena which had already been interpreted in terms of Drift, the hypothesis would have been extremely *ad hoc* with respect to Drift; it would have offered supporters of Drift no more than a solution to one of their more vexing problems, though of course that in itself was no mean achievement .... Holmes, in supplying other consequences of his hypothesis, however, offered adherents of Drift the real bonus of increased explanatory power" (1978: 146).

The fixism/mobilism debate is a good illustration of how different participants in a scientific debate value the theoretical virtues for their ability to promote differing live scientific aims. Even though many of the hypotheses were in direct opposition to each other and several ultimately discarded, their proponents viewed their pursuit as legitimate epistemic endeavours and thought of successfully addressing relevant concerns as notable epistemic achievements. Frankel's analysis makes clear the relative epistemic value of these different goals as well as the epistemic work that the virtues did in pursuit of those aims for the various participants in different stages of this decades-long debate.

3.5 Epistemic Inertness

In the Drift case, it's abundantly clear that the theoretical virtues were doing epistemic *work* in promoting live scientific goals, but this doesn't always have to be the case: the virtues can also be epistemically inert. This is the case when a theory or hypothesis possesses one or several virtues, but in name only, that is, when it 'merely has' a theoretical virtue without that virtue fostering any particular, actual scientific aims. The 'theory' that the tides are caused by fairies is a good, if fanciful, example of this. Imagine magical tide fairies living deep in the ocean, their magic waxing and waning with the phases of the moon. Instead of the moon's and sun's gravitational pull, high tides are said to be actually caused by the fairies, who regularly combine their powers to draw the water towards the shore, with low tides being the result of the fairies communally releasing the water back to sea, perhaps as part of an elaborate dance or game.

While this brief account doesn't contain much detail, it's easy enough to see how one might further elaborate on it without contradicting established scientific knowledge, principles, or evidence. One can also give it explanatory power by making a connection between the tides and the effects of the positions of various celestial bodies on the fairies' magical powers. Nevertheless, it's clear that both consistency with other theories and explanatory power are at most superficial in this case. The theory fails to provide any candidates for plausible mechanisms for the influence of the moon on magic or for the fairies' causal influence on the tides. How are they generating the force to move enormous bodies of water and how do they coordinate their actions globally to create regular tidal patterns? And while the tide fairy theory might be designed to not contradict available knowledge or data, it does not explain the ways in which it is supposedly consistent with either the general laws of physics or more specific principles of oceanography. It might have a high potential for fertility in opening up research into an entirely new domain – fairy magic and powers – but there are no concrete examples of how this alleged fertility is instantiated. One could also argue that the fairy theory has broad scope, because the fairies are responsible not just for the tides, but also other natural phenomena, such as ocean currents, weather patterns, or perhaps even the rotation of the Earth. Yet, it's not possible to point to specific ways in which the fairy theory encompasses such different fields or lines of evidence. Thus, while the fairy theory might be in possession of some virtues, those virtues don't do any work and are epistemically idle.

Of course, one also doesn't want to prejudge the case against the fairies; after all, many of our scientific theories are unintuitive. Thus, if the fairy theory did propose plausible mechanisms – for example, by providing empirical evidence that magic does operate in this realm, by giving a plausible story about the manipulation of water molecules by magic, or an account of how gravitational influences and fluctuations could be magically harnessed in focused ways – it might give rise to hypotheses that are worthy of further investigation. As it stands, however, the puzzles associated with the fairy theory are not live puzzles of any scientific community. Further, whatever exactly the virtues of the fairy theory may be, they do not serve live scientific epistemic aims, such as addressing challenges in predicting tides in areas with complex coastlines, questions about how rising sea levels and changes in ocean currents affect tidal patterns, how the tides could be harnessed in service of renewable energy, or how the tides shape marine ecosystems. If the fairy theory did pursue those goals, we should expect the virtues to become increasingly epistemically plugged into the different parts of the fairy theory in an integral way, with clear examples of how the different virtues would work in service of those aims, just as they did in the continental drift case.

A discussion of who decides what counts as a scientific aim would take us too far afield, so I'll just note that the Epistemic Labour View of Virtues does not require or even presuppose any particular view on this. What matters for its purposes is simply what the present scientific questions are, regardless of their origin. These questions, as well as their associated puzzles and problems are constantly in flux. Sometimes it might not be easy to judge whether a particular question or aim is 'genuinely scientific', but often this judgement can be made in straightforward ways: fairy theories, astrology, flat earth theories, and chemtrail views do not address currently live scientific questions; evolution by natural selection, gravitational tide theories, plate tectonics, general relativity, and the germ theory of disease do, as did theories about phlogiston, the luminiferous aether, and spontaneous generation in their day.

The upshot of this discussion is to illustrate the important distinction the Epistemic Labour View draws between 'merely possessing' a theoretical virtue and that virtue doing genuine epistemic work. The theoretical virtues do such work when they promote real scientific epistemic aims, broadly conceived. Thus, whereas on the traditional realist account, a theory's possessing the virtues signals the approximate truth of that theory, on the Epistemic Labour View a theory's possessing the virtues is not a sign of anything in particular at all – epistemic or otherwise. If, upon further scrutiny, the virtues hold up and are found to do epistemic work, then they're a sign that that theory is making progress towards achieving its scientific epistemic aims. Just how good a theory is in this respect will depend on just how much work the virtues actually do for it.

4 Theoretical Virtues and Underdetermination

4.1 Introduction

In Section 2, we saw that one argument against the truth-conduciveness of the virtues was that pretty much any theory can be made to have some virtues and, further, that realists have trouble comparing theories all of which have virtues. Section 3 developed the Epistemic Labour View of Theoretical Virtues, arguing that the epistemic role of the virtues in a theory depends not on whether that theory possesses virtues but on what work the virtues do in promoting scientific epistemic aims. In this section, I draw these two strands together and show that the virtues aren't truth-conducive even in cases of clearly genuine scientific theories, because they can also function epistemically in completely false theories. I do so via another historical episode, the nineteenth-century debate between miasma and germ theorists about the nature and cause of cholera. In particular, I'll show (i) that the miasma theory cannot be said to be approximately true in any realist sense, but also (ii) that both the miasma and the germ theory not just instantiated the theoretical virtues, but put them to epistemic work in the service of fostering their respective epistemic aims. In fact, the virtues play analogous roles in both theories, and there is thus nothing in particular that the virtues do in true theories that they don't also do in false ones.

Subsection 4.2 will discuss this episode from mid nineteenth-century disease theory, examining both sides of a debate that, arguably, constituted a case of (temporary) underdetermination. I will show that both sides in this debate invoked a number of specific virtues commonly appearing on the realist's list and that they put the virtues to work in distinctly epistemic contexts.

Subsection 4.3 strengthens the conclusions from Section 3, that the theoretical virtues play an epistemic role by doing work in the service of epistemic goals and are therefore not merely pragmatic. Neither, however, are they truth-conducive since, as we will see, even proponents of what turned out to be a completely false theory, relied on these virtues in making their epistemic case. In Subsection 4.4, I will argue that we should generally expect even false theories to exhibit theoretical virtues, thereby undercutting the realist's alleged connection between the virtues and their truth-conduciveness. This ultimately suggests that the right way to approach the virtue question is empirically, through examining cases in the history of science and/or actual science, not through heavily abstract arguments, and also, as we have already stressed, that the question of underdetermination ought to be addressed on a case-by-case basis. Subsection 4.5 highlights the differences between the Epistemic Labour View of Virtues and the standard realist view. I end, in Subsection 4.6, with a discussion of the new role my view carves out for the theoretical virtues, especially in the context of underdetermination.

4.2 Historical Interlude

The historical episode illustrating my points centres around mid nineteenth-century disease theory, in particular around the debate about the origin and transmissibility of cholera. Cholera is an infectious disease of the small intestine, now known to be caused by the bacteria *Vibrio cholerae* and to be transmissible via contaminated water, food, and other materials. It was a dramatic disease, whose initial state manifested as "a sick stomach … vomiting or purging of a liquid like rice-water … [T]he face becomes sharp and shrunken, the eyes sink and look wild, the lips, face and … whole surface of the body [turn] a leaden, blue, purple, [or] black" (Sunderland Herald, October 1831, cited in Dobson 2015: 92). Since there was no known treatment and "King cholera" had a mortality rate of about 50–60 per cent, it was responsible for a significant number of nineteenth-century deaths. Despite its importance, there was much confusion about cholera: "Is it a fungus, an insect, a miasma, an electrical disturbance, a deficiency of ozone, a morbid offscouring of the intestinal canal? We know nothing; we are at sea in a whirlpool of conjecture" (The Lancet II, 393, 1853; also quoted in Vinten-Johansen et al. 2003: 166). And while there were a number of different accounts potentially addressing various aspects of cholera, two emerged as the main competitors in terms of seeking to explain disease origin and transmissibility: first, the miasma theory of disease and second, John Snow's famous water hypothesis.

Briefly, according to the miasma theory, miasmas that were the result of rotting and decomposing organic matter would be suspended in the air, enter individuals via inhalation or direct contact, and then be absorbed by the blood where they would essentially set off something akin to a pathological decomposition process in those affected. Cholera, according to this picture, was not thought of as a particular substance but instead as a transformative chemical process akin to fermentation. While there were in principle multiple ways in which cholera could be contracted, the main route was thought to be through contaminated air, with various weather and atmospheric conditions as well as potential victims' personal characteristics and constitution affecting who would fall sick and how severely. The causal picture underlying the miasma theory involved both a number of different causes (air, water, etc.) as well as different types of causes (predisposing, exciting, mixed, etc.).

Snow's theory, in contrast, was monocausal and proposed contaminated water as the main driver of cholera transmission, through "the mixture of the cholera evacuations with the water used for drinking and culinary purposes, either by permeating the ground, and getting into wells, or by running along channels and sewers into the rivers from which entire towns are some times supplied" (1855: 22–23). Snow first articulated this view in his famous *On the Mode of Communication of Cholera* (1849), producing a much expanded edition in 1855. Unlike the miasmatists, Snow posited "that the morbid material producing cholera must be introduced into the alimentary canal" (1855: 15). Since the miasmatists accepted many potential causes of cholera, they were not opposed to water transmission in principle. The difference to Snow was, as he explained, that "many medical men, whilst they admit the influence of polluted water on the prevalence of cholera, believe that it acts by predisposing or preparing the system to be acted on by some unknown cause of the disease existing in the atmosphere or elsewhere ... that opinion cannot long halt here ... if the effect of contaminated water be admitted, it must lead to the conclusion that it acts by containing the true and specific cause of the malady" (1855: 110).

As we can see, these two accounts are quite different, one viewing cholera as a chemical process with air as the dominant transmission route, the other viewing cholera as caused by a waterborne ingested agent. And while Snow turned out to be right in the end, and this might seem obvious to us now, in the mid nineteenth century this was far from clear. In fact, this situation might plausibly be construed as a case of temporary underdetermination (according to the original underdetermination argument), since at the time the empirical evidence was the same for everyone but did not clearly single out one of these two options as superior. Can the theoretical virtues break the tie?

Although much more can be said about the reasoning of the miasmatists (Tulodziecki 2016a, 2016b, 2017a, 2017b, 2021) and Snow (see Tulodziecki 2011, 2012b, 2013, 2019), let's for now pick out a couple of theoretical virtues that commonly appear on realists' lists, focusing on two especially important to many realists: explanatory power and a theory's ability to generate novel predictions. Let's start with Snow and explanatory power. Snow's account does well in this respect. For example, it could explain the high incidence of cholera in certain demographic groups that, according to the miasma theory, should not have been particularly susceptible. One such class were miners. Since there are no sources of miasmas underground, they should not have had unusually high rates of cholera, yet they did. Snow's explanation is that "[t]here are neither privies, hand-basins, nor towels in the mines; and when a case of cholera occurs in a pit, the hands of the workmen, in the dark subterranean passages, can hardly fail to become soiled with the discharges" (1851: 560a). Moreover, since miners spent their entire day below ground, including consuming food and drink, this provided optimal conditions for cholera to be transmitted 'from one intestine to another'. Snow also thought he could explain how cholera became epidemic – through heavily used contaminated public water supplies. Further, he could explain how people initially unconnected to a particular outbreak ended up contracting the disease. In the case of the famous Broad Street Pump, for example, to which the 1854 Soho outbreak was eventually traced, Snow ended up linking a number of non-local victims to the pump water, through routes such as pubs that used pump water for mixing drinks, or coffeehouses and restaurants that served pump water with their meals. Snow could also explain why certain locations that should have been particularly prone to cholera according to the miasmas theory, ended up with comparatively little. For example, poorhouse inhabitants were thought to exhibit a number of characteristics that should have predisposed them to diseases, including cholera, such as generally poor morals and the conditions of the poorhouse itself, involving poor nutrition and hygiene. Snow, however, found out that the inmates did not receive their water from the Broad Street pump. Similarly, the brewery, despite being located in the middle of an outbreak zone, hardly had any cholera victims. Besides having its own well, Snow also found that the workers were "allowed a certain quantity of malt liquor, and Mr. Huggins believes they do not drink water at all" (1855: 2).

Let's turn next to a theory's ability to make novel predictions. This is viewed by many realists as the hallmark of genuine scientific success and therefore a popular theoretical virtue. Snow's account, it turns out, does well in this respect, too. Among other things, he predicted that ingesting water contaminated with the cholera poison would mean a higher risk of contracting cholera and that disease incidence and mortality should be especially high around contaminated sources. More generally, he was able to predict where one should and shouldn't expect to find high mortality rates, that where mortality rates were low within an affected area, there would be alternative water sources, and so on. Snow also managed to predict certain epidemiological patterns, such as that cholera mortality was much higher at the beginning of outbreaks before tapering off (for more, see Tulodziecki 2016a). Lastly, one of his most famous predictions was the expected outcome of the famous "natural experiment" now known as the South London water study. Here, Snow attempted to show that differential cholera mortality in South London during the 1853–1854 epidemic depended on which water company supplied one's water. His "experiment" capitalized on the fact that South London contained a district, supplied by two different water companies, the Lambeth Company and the Southwark & Vauxhall Company. The former drew its water from an upstream, less polluted part of the Thames, whereas the latter drew its water from a highly polluted downstream location. The fact that the district was supplied by both companies resulted in "a population of 300,000 persons, of various conditions and occupations, intimately mixed together, and divided into two groups by no other circumstance than the difference of water supply" (Snow 1856: 241–242). Snow predicted that cholera incidence and mortality rates ought to differ depending on one's water source and turned out to be right. This experiment is often regarded as a pivotal experiment in the history of epidemiology and Snow's prediction is regarded by many as one of Snow's greatest successes (for some problems with this view, however, see Parkes 1855, Eyler 2013, Koch 2013, Tulodziecki 2019).

Nonetheless, just like Snow's account, the miasma theory also had its successes and did well with respect to both of the aforementioned virtues. It, too, exhibited a high degree of explanatory power. As we already saw, the miasma theory relied on the idea that miasmas were produced by decomposing materials. It followed, therefore, that conditions for putrefaction and cholera incidence and mortality ought to be tied together and one ought to expect more cholera when the conditions were favourable to miasmas. It was this link to sources of decomposition that allowed the miasma theory to give successful explanations of a number of cholera-related phenomena. For example, it could explain seasonal disease outbreaks and why cholera incidence and mortality were particularly high during periods of hot weather. Elevated temperatures and higher humidity facilitate the decomposition of organic matter, thereby providing particularly favourable conditions for the production of miasmas. It further explained why certain geographical regions and locations, such as marshy areas, urban centres, barracks, and prisons, and more densely populated areas in general were particularly vulnerable. These areas were both high in sources of decomposing organic matter, especially sewage and waste, but they were also badly ventilated, which meant that miasmas generated by refuse would linger and be unable to disperse. It could also explain why, despite no prior contact with previous victims, cholera could appear suddenly and move around, since sources of decomposing matter don't require other, already existing sources and can arise and turn into miasmatic sources in isolation. It was thus possible for miasmas to be present in otherwise healthy areas and in this way they could cause highly localized outbreaks, but also potentially cause disease in larger regions where one might not otherwise expect it. Merthyr-Tydfil, a town in Wales, was such an example. Despite being in what should have been a location with little expected disease, "some parts of town are complete networks of filth emitting noxious exhalations", which accounted for its unusually high mortality (Farr 1852: liv). The miasma theory could also explain why quarantines failed to prevent the disease from spreading – it is possible to quarantine people, but not moving air arising from sources of decomposition. Lastly, it managed to explain individual variations in susceptibility, through giving a chemical account of how different individuals' blood reacted when exposed (see Farr 1842, Liebig 1842, Hamlin 1982: 93ff., Tulodziecki 2016a). This chemical account was well-suited here, since it was based on the idea that a victim's blood would transform upon contracting the disease. This provided an explanation for why certain diseases tended to only affect children – adult blood lacked the prerequisite material required for the relevant transformation – and for why certain diseases could only be contracted once – the required pre-existing material in the blood gets transformed and used up when one falls ill the first time, and there is thus nothing left to initiate a second round.

The miasma theory also did well with respect to generating novel predictions. So-called use-novel predictions are of particular interest in this context, since, as we saw, this is the criterion realists tend to cite as the hallmark of genuine scientific success. A prediction is use-novel when it is not used in the construction of the theory it seeks to support, excluding the possibility that the theory was constructed specifically around the prediction, in which case the prediction could not then also function as confirmation of that theory. The miasma theory, perhaps surprisingly, could deliver on this front. It *followed* from the miasma theory that there should be a correlation between sources of miasma and air quality and on that basis the miasma theory was able to make a number of specific predictions about air quality in different locations. For example, it predicted that air quality ought to be better in areas with fewer sources of miasma, such as the highlands, and worse as the number of those sources (i.e., rotting organic material) increased, as was the case for low-lying riverbanks, swamps, marshes, stagnant or polluted bodies of water, poorly maintained wells, open sewers, overflowing cesspools, and, in general, areas where human and animal waste accumulated.[26] The miasma theory also included predictions about the amount of organic material one should expect to see in different types of air and predictions about how this should correlate with disease incidence and mortality. These predictions were confirmed by chemists at the time and should therefore, according to the realist's own criterion, count as genuine successes for the miasma theory (for more detail, see Tulodziecki 2017b). In a similar vein, the miasma theory made use-novel predictions about the relationship between cholera incidence and weather and atmospheric conditions, population density, different occupations, as well as predictions about the course and duration of various epidemics.

Its crowning achievement, however, were William Farr's specific and highly impressive predictions about the prevalence of cholera at different elevations. Farr (1807–1883) was the statistical superintendent of the General Register Office from 1842 to 1879. He found that "mortality from cholera is in the inverse ratio of the elevation" (Farr 1852: lxi) and managed to generate an equation capturing the exact relationship between increased soil elevation and the decline of cholera, which he subsequently confirmed to an astonishing degree. Farr's Elevation Law stands out, not just because it was mathematically precise and as good a prediction as any disease theory could be expected to produce, but also because it was much more specific than anything any of his competitors, including Snow, had to offer. It supplied for the first time a quantifiable prediction that, moreover, was found to stand up to testing. When the American epidemiologist Alexander Langmuir – whose credentials include serving for over two decades as the Chief Epidemiologist for the CDC and developing the CDC's Epidemic Intelligence Service training program – plotted Farr's results in 1961, he was still impressed with just how good Farr's predictions were, calling Farr's results "a confirmation that I believe would be impressive to any scientist at any time" (173).[27]

4.3 Cholera and Theoretical Virtues

So, as we can see, both Snow's and the miasmatists' accounts instantiated some of the theoretical virtues valued most highly by realists. Both do well with

---

[26] Of course, knowing, as we do now, that cholera is a disease passed from intestine to intestine, it is not surprising that its incidence would be higher close to contaminated drinking water and areas that tended to be on the receiving end of human excreta, especially in combination (such as cesspools leaking into drinking water, as in the famous Broad Street Pump episode).

[27] Eventually the law was found not to hold up. I discuss the Elevation Law as well as possible objections to it in the context of the realism debate in more detail in Tulodziecki (2021).

respect to explanatory power and novel predictions, the miasma theory despite the fact that it turned out to be false. There are also a number of other virtues that they both exhibited, to different degrees at different times. The miasma theory in its mid nineteenth-century heyday did well with respect to coherence with other established theories and fruitfulness. It cohered especially well with prominent chemical theories, such as that by Justus von Liebig (1803–1873), who didn't just try to give accounts of processes such as decomposition, but also had his own miasmatic pathology. Liebig's theories were already both well-known as well as highly successful in agriculture and miasmatic disease theories seemed to fit well into this overall framework, with potential and promising explanations of how the environment and individual people interacted to produce disease (Farr 1852: lxxx–lxxxiii). This, however, changed over the course of the next several decades; with the germ theory of disease beginning to gain a foothold, the situation began to reverse. Similar points can be made about several other theoretical virtues and with respect to both Snow and the miasmatists.

It's also clear that both Snow and his opponents regarded the virtues as playing an epistemically significant role in their theorizing. For example, with respect to explanatory power Snow explicitly states that "there are certain circumstances connected with the history of cholera which admit of a satisfactory explanation according to these principles explained above [i.e., Snow's account of cholera], and [that] consequently tend to confirm those principles" (1855: 115). Farr similarly stressed the importance of explanatory power, as did other prominent cholera experts at the time. E.A. Parkes, for example, a notable critic of Snow, criticized Snow's views on the grounds that his explanations were much less impressive than Snow claimed. He also pointed to Snow's failure to respond to objections as well as his failure to discuss rival explanations, especially Farr's elevation hypothesis (Eyler 2013, Koch 2013, Tulodziecki 2019). But Parkes and others were not opposed to Snow's account in general; they just disagreed with Snow about how good an explanation he in fact provided. Parkes even went so far as to state explicitly that "when additional evidence shall be given, we shall receive it with the greatest pleasure; for though we think Dr. Snow's hypothesis, if proved, cannot explain all the phenomena of the spread of cholera, it would yet clear up some of the mysterious phenomena of its diffusion. Its establishment would therefore be an immense gain to science, and, we need not add, an important service to the State" (1855: 462–463). When that evidence finally came in both Parkes and Farr adjusted their views and Farr played a crucial role in helping to gather data during the 1866 London epidemic that would support Snow's views.

There was thus a lively debate about the explanatory power of the various cholera hypotheses. The important takeaway for our purposes is that everyone agreed that explanatory power was epistemically important, they just disagreed about which account fared best and about the extent to which the available evidence supported the various explanatory claims. Thus, the problem at the time was that it simply wasn't clear who did better and as a result there was underdetermination not just with respect to the empirical evidence, but also with respect to explanatory power itself. The reason this was such a difficult issue to resolve was twofold: first, there were a number of phenomena everyone agreed stood in need of an explanation but that were explained by only one of the parties; second, the miasmatists and Snow had somewhat different explananda and therefore different scientific goals. For example, live goals for Snow, but not the miasmatists, were providing an explanation for why not everyone who drank cholera-contaminated water contracted the disease and an account of those deaths that had no connection to polluted water. Live goals for the miasmatists, but not Snow, were to address various questions about air quality and airborne transmission. This shows that the point of Section 2 is not just theoretical; difficulties in comparing theories both of which have virtues are real. And this is not just a retroactive problem arising long after the fact. In this case, the most qualified cholera experts at the time disagreed about which account was superior.

Realists might reply that nobody is denying that there can be real cases of temporary underdetermination and that that is all we are seeing here. While this is true, this is not all the cholera case shows. Instead, there are two main points here: first, that it's not clear or straightforward how the theoretical virtues can break cases of underdetermination in situations like these, when both parties are pursuing somewhat different aims; second, that cases such as these sever the alleged link between the theoretical virtues and (approximate) truth that realists require in order for the theoretical virtues to be epistemic. Remember that for realists the virtues' being epistemic amounts to their being truth-conducive and that the idea behind their objection to the ECT was that theories that have the virtues are more likely to be true than virtues not having them. Thus, prima facie, the Snow case looks exactly like the sort of case realists like. After all, Snow's view turned out to be correct and so it looks like a good candidate for beginning to make an argument for the truth-conduciveness of the theoretical virtues: Snow did appeal to several virtues, these virtues played an epistemic role for him, and he got things more or less right. The problem for realists is that the main rival view to Snow's also instantiated and put to work the theoretical virtues. Thus, in the cholera case we have two rival theories, both of which put virtues to work in promoting their respective epistemic goals, but that are also incompatible with each other, so they can't both be true. Yet, if the virtues are truly truth-conducive, they should be truth-conducive in both cases.

Realists might try to respond that Snow got it right, but that, still, the miasma theory was approximately true and that therefore its having the virtues does not speak against the truth-conduciveness of the virtues more generally. In the case of the miasma theory, however, the case for approximate truth is hard to make since none of the usual candidates for approximate truth – in particular, none of the elements responsible for the miasma theory's successes – were retained. Its laws and mechanisms were discarded; neither are there structural features that were carried over to any of its successors. Most crucially, the miasma theory's successor did not contain anything like miasmas, even though miasmas had a central role both in the aetiology and transmission of cholera; neither did it contain anything that can reasonably be said to have the same properties that miasmas did. As a result, the miasma theory does not contain any candidates for approximate truth (for more detail on this, see Tulodziecki 2016a, 2017b). Lastly, the miasmatists conceived of cholera as the result of chemical transformations whereas the germ theory conceived of cholera as the result of a pathogenic, biological microorganism. This shift from the chemical to the biological is as large a conceptual shift in this domain as is possible, and if it's possible to make the case for approximate truth here, one should be able to make the case for the approximate truth of pretty much any two scientific theories, regardless of how different they are. Thus, things don't look good for the potential realist response that holds that the miasma theory was, after all, approximately true.

But even if the miasma theory *were* approximately true, this would not help realists with respect to underdetermination. In the case of Snow and the miasmatists, we had two opposing camps, with two incompatible pictures of disease transmission. In the 1840s and 1850s, these two theories, for all practical purposes, could be regarded as empirically equivalent. According to the realist, the theoretical virtues are supposed to help us out of underdetermination scenarios by breaking the tie, precisely because the virtues are truth-conducive and so allegedly point the way to that theory that is more likely to be approximately true. But if a theory and its rival – one that is incompatible – can now both be approximately true, even though at least one of them is definitely false, approximate truth can no longer fulfil the function for which realists introduced it in the first place. After all, approximately true theories are supposed to be those 'on the way to truth' and if theories and their direct and false competitors can both be approximately true, the idea of approximate truth loses much of its bite. Moreover, if the virtues can point to two incompatible theories, at least one of which is definitely false, it's hard to see in what sense they can be said to be truth-conducive at this point. Or, more strongly: if theories as false as the miasma theory could help establish the truth-conduciveness of the virtues, truth-conduciveness is no longer anything of practical epistemic significance, since almost anything could then be truth-conduciveness in some fashion or another. But either way, the theoretical virtues don't help us pick one way or the other. And so regardless of whether the miasma theory is approximately true or not, if theories that didn't turn out to be correct also have theoretical virtues, the virtues simply aren't up to the job they were supposed to do.

4.4 Theoretical Virtues, False Theories, and Realism

One might try to argue that even if both theories are approximately true, Snow's is *more* likely to be approximately true. In this vein, realists might devote some time trying to produce an argument that shows that Snow's account really was epistemically superior. I have no doubt that this is possible. But I also have no doubt that someone equally devoted could produce an analogous story about the miasmatists. And while we might be able to make such arguments retroactively, it's clear that at least in this case this will not be achieved through just appealing to the virtues. Moreover, the fact that even the world's experts at the time disagreed, when there was and is nobody more qualified to adjudicate, either then or now, should give us further pause.

Next, someone might try to argue that this case is atypical and that there is no reason to think that other cases would be similar in nature. That's possible, but even if true, the cholera episode nevertheless illustrates how difficult it is to compare theories with respect to the virtues. This goes especially for explanatory power, in which the two competitors had somewhat different explananda. In order to make comparisons of explanatory power in such situations, one needs to invoke something beyond the virtues in order to arbitrate how well they do in this respect. Perhaps each side thinks their own respective explananda stand in greater need of explanation. But such holistic judgements about what is most urgent or important to address at a particular time go beyond the debate just about the theoretical virtues. In the case of Snow and the miasmatists, for example, the fact that they held mono- and multicausal disease frameworks, respectively, certainly influenced the questions they asked and what they took to be central puzzles in need of solving. In 3.4, we saw that this was also a feature of the continental drift debate, with fixists and mobilists each privileging and pursuing somewhat different sets of questions. Moreover, the fact that the history of science is full of genuine debates among bona fide experts – about the existence of the luminiferous aether, about phlogiston, about the nature of light, about whether life could arise spontaneously, and so on – suggests that these cases are not isolated examples. If there had been an obviously epistemically superior option in those cases, one would expect experts to have recognized this instead of spending several decades arguing. After all, the debates in these cases were among respected scientists on all sides. Snow's name might be the one more widely recognized today, but Farr is considered the founder of vital statistics, and Snow's critic Parkes authored the first public health textbook.

It's true that Snow ended up winning out, but he did so only after decades of debate, when the situation with respect to empirical evidence as well as with respect to instruments and techniques had undergone significant developments. As a result of these discussions, more data and evidence, and new types of analyses, people eventually – and gradually – converged on what we now think of as the right position. The point here is that, during much of this time, things were genuinely open, up in the air, and there simply was no one option that was clearly superior to the other(s). Both theories exhibited a number of virtues, both sides agreed these virtues did important work in furthering their respective epistemic goals, and both sides thought that their option was, on balance, the better one. What changed during these decades of debate is not so much what virtues were had by what theories, but the degrees to which people thought these theories instantiated their virtues, and to what degree the virtues were involved in promoting changing scientific aims. With more evidence, changing explananda, and new ways to test hypotheses, the balance gradually shifted from – initially – the miasma over the water hypothesis, through a murkier period where the balance was not clear, to – eventually – the water over the miasma hypothesis. Frankel's analysis tells a similar story about continental drift (2012). Thus, as I already suggested before, even when the virtues have epistemic impact, that impact is not simply a matter of a theory's having or not having a virtue. The very same theory might possess the same virtue – possibly over decades – as in the cases earlier, and yet the degree of epistemic contribution that virtue makes to that theory's epistemic standing might vary greatly at different times as the theory evolves and different puzzles and problems take centre stage. The degree to which Snow's theory exemplified its virtues was highly dynamic and changed over time. The virtues it had in the 1890s were not the same ones it had in the 1840s, even though, technically, they were the same in name. Comparing two snapshots of its explanatory power, one taken in 1840 and one in 1890, reveals an enormous difference; but focusing only on the 1890s snapshot will tell a misleading story about the epistemic power of Snow's theory, even if it turned out to be correct in the end. What this shows is that taking a synchronic snapshot of a theory's 'virtue status' – whether it's the 'winning' or 'losing' theory – is not helpful. There is no matter of fact about how miasmatic or water views did with respect to the virtues *simpliciter*.

Instead, the question is to what extent these virtues promoted changing goals, and how they were weighed at different times and in relation to whatever competitors were serious contenders. For simplicity's sake, I have only mentioned Farr and Snow with respect to cholera but there were other options on the table, such as Budd's fungal theory (Hamlin 2009).

The other important take-away from this episode is that looking at any one theory in isolation – Farr's, Snow's, others' – and what virtues that theory exhibits can't tell us that much about the epistemic standing of that theory. Snow's water hypothesis ended up winning the day, as did Wegener's drift hypothesis. But if we want to know why they did so, pointing to their virtues at a particular point in time will not give us the answer. It's important to know that they exhibited several virtues, of course, but we can shed light on its epistemic status only by appropriately contextualizing it. How well a given theory instantiates a particular virtue at a particular time and how well that virtue promotes scientific goals, depends on extra-theoretical circumstances, and there is thus no way of making the relevant virtue-assessments without understanding what else was going on. If we just look at Snow, we can make a case that his view scored extremely high on explanatory power (see Tulodziecki 2011 for an account along these lines), but once we take into account the successes of Farr and the criticism of Parkes, things look much less good for Snow. How strong Snow's theory is in terms of explanatory power depends at least in part on the epistemic power of other accounts at the time. In hindsight, such (ultimately losing) explanations are often underestimated, as was the case with the miasma theory, not least because all too often our narratives focus on those theories that won out in the end. Perhaps the most important takeaway therefore is that it is disingenuous to insist that just because the situation at some point clearly favoured many of Snow's claims (as later acknowledged by Farr and Parkes), Snow was always the clearly superior option to begin with.

In short, during the periods of intense debate, there was underdetermination not just with respect to the evidence, but also with respect to the virtues, and it was unclear how to resolve it. Both sides in this debate (and the many 'sides' in between) agreed on the importance of many of the theoretical virtues, but they disagreed about the degree to which the various options instantiated them, as well as to what extent those virtues promoted relevant goals.[28] But this is exactly how it should be. It's precisely the fact that both options exhibited some of the virtues and put the virtues to serious epistemic work that made it

---

[28] Worboys (2000: 278) has stressed that there were many different versions of miasmatism and germ views in the nineteenth century and that it is misleading to think of a unified germ theory at this time; see also Hamlin (2009).

unclear who, if anyone, did better, and that therefore made this a genuine scientific debate.

We should expect false or rejected theories that were (or are) seriously in the running among relevant groups of experts to exhibit more or less the same properties as those that end up surviving. It's because all options do well with respect to what is valued that such debates take place. If this weren't the case the debates themselves would be puzzling, perpetuating a perplexing picture of otherwise excellent scientists who simply couldn't recognize what was apparently relatively clear, at least to the lone, trailblazing genius who won the day (and in whose footsteps we are stepping now). Moreover, let's not forget that many now discarded theories were at some point the best available ones, many for decades or even centuries. Newtonian Mechanics dominated for a long time and this would have been surprising, had it not been both extremely successful and had many of the properties that we take to be indicative of this success. Just like Newton's, Einstein's picture might get replaced. Still, it is awfully good and we should expect it to have all the epistemic criteria we associate with excellent science, regardless of whether at some point in the future it will be judged to be approximately true by philosophers or not. That the virtues make it more likely to be true than not could be established only if we could assess independently whether there is a connection between the theoretical virtues and approximate truth. Given that we just saw that false theories also exhibit the virtues, the prospects for that argument aren't good. But that should not call into question the terrific epistemic achievements of many of our past, false theories, and sometimes even the achievements of those theories that never ended up being accepted, but were only temporary participants during periods of intense debate.

4.5 The Epistemic Labour View vs. the Realist View of Virtues

The upshot of this historical discussion is that the fact that the miasma theory instantiated and put to work theoretical virtues undercuts the realist claim that the theoretical virtues are truth-conducive. While we could perhaps try to argue for their truth-conduciveness based on an examination of Snow, what this overall discussion brings out is that realists, in order to make that argument, require a lot more. In particular, it's not enough for realists to adduce cases of approximately true theories that were arrived at by invoking the virtues, or that instantiate the virtues. They also require that this be the case *only* for (approximately) true theories (or for most of them, at any rate). After all, if false theories instantiate the virtues just as much, it's hard to see how the virtues are conducing towards the truth, since they sometimes conduce to falsity. And, since we don't know which of these two situations we are in, the virtues cannot help break ties in underdetermination scenarios.

But we should not conclude from this that the virtues play no epistemic role whatsoever, as anti-realists claim. As we saw, all sides in the cholera debate put the virtues to work in service of their respective aims and viewed at least some theoretical virtues as conferring epistemic power on their various claims. Both Snow and the miasmatists had a number of distinctly epistemological achievements in their favour. Among other things, they both showed how to bring to bear methods and methodology from one domain into another (integrating, in various ways, pathology, statistics, and epidemiology), they both tried to subsume phenomena under laws, they both attempted to construct models, they both had as an important goal increasing understanding, they both tried to identify causally relevant factors and relations, they both tried to identify, classify, and relate various variables to each other. Farr even explicitly tried to mathematize the domain of diseases.

Cases like these speak directly against the standard realist view of the virtues and make clear that the virtues are not signs of (approximate) truth. Unlike realists, proponents of the Epistemic Labour View don't require a systematic connection between the theoretical virtues and truth (or any other epistemic aim) in order for the virtues to play an epistemic role. The need for such a connection is the source of the realist's vulnerability to historical arguments showing that a theory's having virtues is compatible with its falsity. In contrast, the Epistemic Labour View doesn't just expect false theories to have working virtues, but explains *why* we should expect this. Past theories that were taken to be serious competitors over prolonged periods of time lasted precisely because they had epistemic successes, with the virtues helping to promote relevant epistemic goals. The Epistemic Labour View also explains how a theory's virtue assessment can change over time as well as why different people might produce differing assessments at the same point in time. For one, epistemic aims are not fixed or static over a theory's life and so how well a virtue promotes live goals changes as both the theory and its goals evolve. A theory's ability to unify disparate phenomena might be very impressive in its early stage, when no other competitor can do so, but that very same unification might do much less work at a later time when all candidates do well on this front, and unification no longer plays a central role in promoting its new and changed goals. For another, different scientists, regardless of whether they are in a competing or the same research programme, have different goals, explaining why they might value different virtues to different degrees.

We also saw that a further source of trouble for realists is that pretty much any theory, including non-scientific theories of various ilks, can be made to have at least some virtues, suggesting that simply instantiating the virtues is not enough for them to have epistemic impact. Note that this particular issue is a problem not just for the realist, but for any account that holds that the mere having of the virtues is a sign of epistemic value, whether via truth or some other epistemic notion. Any account according to which simple possession of the virtues signals any kind of epistemic success will have to account for cases widely considered non-genuine. Such cases are notoriously hard to deal with, but adopting the Epistemic Labour View can tackle them by arguing that in such cases the theoretical virtues are epistemically inert. It thus has the resources to explain how it's possible for certain theories to lack epistemic credentials, even when they exhibit theoretical virtues, perhaps even virtues that count as highly desirable on the old view.

4.6 Roles for the Theoretical Virtues

Over the course of this Element, I have argued that the theoretical virtues can't do the realist's job. First, they are not truth-conducive. Second, any theory will possess some virtues, and so if possession of the virtues is the relevant criterion – as it is for realists – realists require a systematic and principled way to rank the virtues, which, I have argued, is impossible. Third, realists run into trouble with the history of science, where scientific debates and controversies make clear that even completely false theories – theories that cannot in any way be said to be approximately true on any of the usual realist accounts – exhibit virtues. What's more, the virtues do serious epistemic work in those cases; they are routinely used to promote live scientific epistemic goals and scientists regularly value them for this ability. Where does this leave us with respect to the theoretical virtues? If they can't do the realist's job, what role do they play? And where are we left with respect to underdetermination?

We saw that the Epistemic Labour View of Virtues shifts the focus away from their possession to whether or not they do epistemic work. This carves out a new role for the virtues in helping us delineate the space of genuine scientific rivals. Only theories instantiating the virtues should even be in the running but, as we saw merely 'having' the virtues is not enough. Instead, the role of the virtues is to contribute to genuinely epistemic aims through addressing genuinely epistemic problems that are in need of solving. The virtues point to serious scientific contenders when they play a role in addressing actual scientific predicaments and when they are put to active use in achieving real and live epistemic goals, however diverse those goals may be. We can get "fairies cause cholera" to instantiate some of the virtues, but even if we do, they don't further solutions to any of the live puzzles faced by anyone working on cholera in the mid-1800s. When the virtues are epistemically inert in this way, this is reason to doubt that we have a scientific theory of interest on our hands. In this way, the virtues can help us sort the scientific wheat from the pseudoscientific chaff.

An almost accidental by-product of this role is that the virtues are able to settle what we might consider 'boring' cases of underdetermination, in which the 'rivals' consist of fairy theories, algorithmically generated competitors, sceptical hypotheses, pseudoscience, conspiracy theories, and the like. Here, the Epistemic Labour conception gives not just the right answer, but also a *reason* for why the alleged underdetermination was never scientifically genuine in the first place: even when such theories possess theoretical virtues, the virtues don't do epistemic work for them, and they were therefore never on an epistemic par with actual scientific theories to begin with.

What about cases in which the virtues do promote scientific epistemic aims? In that event, we can sometimes, but not always, use them to assess our theories' epistemic value. This is perhaps easiest to see through an analogy: take two restaurants with different cuisines. They might use different ingredients, similar ingredients in similar ways, or similar ingredients in different ways. Even though the restaurants are very different, we can sometimes easily determine which of the two is better, because some restaurants are simply terrible while others are outstanding. At other times, it might be impossible to make such a judgement, and perhaps even to compare them. We might recognize both as good on their own terms, but still have a strong preference for one, simply because we value its cuisine more than the other's. We might even give arguments for our preference (Their food is so wonderfully spicy!), as might someone who prefers the competitor (We love how mild their food is!). Just as was the case in the early days of the drift and cholera debates, there simply is no matter of fact that clearly settles the issue. And just like merely having a particular dish on the menu doesn't do anything for a restaurant (it needs to be executed well, too), merely having a virtue doesn't make a theory epistemically valuable. Virtues, just like dishes, have to actively contribute to excellence in order to add value. Lastly, just like we should expect restaurants listed in food guides to have at least some good dishes, we should expect theories from the history of science that were around for significant periods of time to have done well with respect to the virtues, regardless of whether they ultimately turned out to be true, approximately true, or completely false. Such theories lasted precisely because they did well, at least for a time, in addressing live epistemic issues and concerns.

Where does all this leave us with respect to underdetermination? It's unlikely that the virtues can help break live cases, that is, temporary cases in which there is real controversy and dispute, not just about the science but also about the relative importance of the virtues themselves. In such cases, eventually one theory wins out, and at that point we should also expect the theoretical virtues to do more epistemic work for that theory than for its competitor. Thus, if it's relatively clear-cut that a theory and its virtues do better with respect to each other than is the case for any other theory, that is an indicator that the first theory is indeed epistemically superior. However, at that point the virtues don't play a tie-breaking role as much as they are indicators that a scientific consensus is forming or that a debate has come to an end.

Nevertheless, even during periods of underdetermination the theoretical virtues are still able to guide inquiry, helping us figure out where to focus our research and pointing to ways in which particular aims might be achieved. Notably, they can do so for several opposing theories at once. In this way, even without truth, they can guide the development and refinement of existing theories, precisely because they are valued and recognized for their ability to promote the achievement of the many and varied epistemic goals of science.

References

Belot, G. (2015). Down to Earth Underdetermination. *Philosophy and Phenomenological Research*, **91**(2), 456–464.

Bhakthavatsalam, S., & Cartwright, N. (2017). What's So Special about Empirical Adequacy? *European Journal for Philosophy of Science*, 7(3), 445–465.

Biddle, J. (2013). State of the Field: Transient Underdetermination and Values in Science. *Studies in History and Philosophy of Science Part A*, **44**(1), 124–133.

Boyd, R. (1991). Observations, Explanatory Power, and Simplicity: Toward a Non-Humean Account. In R. Boyd, P. Gasper, & J. D. Trout, eds., *The Philosophy of Science*, Cambridge, MA: MIT Press, 349–377.

Bueno, O., & Shalkowski, S. A. (2020). Troubles with Theoretical Virtues: Resisting Theoretical Utility Arguments in Metaphysics. *Philosophy and Phenomenological Research*, **101**(2), 456–469.

Cartwright, N., Hardie, J., Montuschi, E., Soleiman, M., & Thresher, A. C. (2022). *The Tangle of Science*, Oxford: Oxford University Press.

Chakravartty, A. (2017). Scientific Realism. In E. Zalta, ed., *The Stanford Encyclopedia of Philosophy* (Summer Edition). https://plato.stanford.edu/archives/sum2017/entries/scientific-realism/.

Chang, H. (2005). A Case for Old-Fashioned Observability, and a Reconstructed Constructive Empiricism. *Philosophy of Science*, **72**(5), 876–887.

Chang, H. (2018). Is Pluralism Compatible with Scientific Realism? In J. Saatsi, ed., *The Routledge Handbook of Scientific Realism*. New York: Routledge, 176–186.

Chang, H. (2022). *Realism for Realistic People*, Cambridge: Cambridge University Press.

Churchland, P. M. & Hooker, C. A. (eds.) (1985). *Images of Science: Essays on Realism and Empiricism*. Chicago: University of Chicago Press.

Cleland, C. E. (2002). Methodological and Epistemic Differences between Historical Science and Experimental Science. *Philosophy of Science*, **69**(3), 447–451.

Currie, A. (2018). *Rock, Bone, and Ruin*, Cambridge, MA: The MIT Press.

Dawid, R. (2006). Underdetermination and Theory Succession from the Perspective of String Theory. *Philosophy of Science*, **73**(3), 298–322.

De Regt, H. W., & Gijsbers, V. (2016). How False Theories Can Yield Genuine Understanding. In S. Grimm, C. Baumberger, S. Ammon, eds., *Explaining*

Understanding: New Perspectives from Epistemology and Philosophy of Science, London: Routledge, 50–75.

Dobson, M. (2015). *Murderous Contagion: A Human History of Disease*, London: Quercus.

Duhem, P. M. M. (1954 [1906]). *The Aim and Structure of Physical Theory*, Princeton: Princeton University Press.

Earman, J. (1993). Underdetermination, Realism, and Reason. *Midwest Studies in Philosophy*, **18**, 19–38.

Egg, M., & Saatsi, J. (2021). Scientific Realism and Underdetermination in Quantum Theory. *Philosophy Compass*, **16**(11), e12773.

Eyler, J. (2013). Commentary: Confronting Unexpected Results: Edmund Parkes Reviews John Snow. *International Journal of Epidemiology*, **42**(6), 1559–1562.

Farr, W. (1842). *Fourth Annual Report to the Registrar General*, London: W. Clowes.

Farr, W. (1852). *Report on the Mortality of Cholera in England, 1848–49*, London: W. Clowes and Sons.

Frank, P. (1957). *Philosophy of Science*, Englewood Cliffs: Prentice-Hall.

Frankel, H. (1976). Alfred Wegener and the Specialists. *Centaurus*, **20**(4), 305–324.

Frankel, H. (1978). Arthur Holmes and Continental Drift. *The British Journal for the History of Science*, **11**(2), 130–150.

Frankel, H. R. (2012). *The Continental Drift Controversy (4 Volumes)*, Cambridge: Cambridge University Press.

Fraser, D. (2009). Quantum Field Theory: Underdetermination, Inconsistency, and Idealization. *Philosophy of Science*, **76**(4), 536–567.

Hamlin, C. (1982). *What Becomes of Pollution?* Doctoral Dissertation. Madison: University of Wisconsin-Madison.

Hamlin, C. (2009). *Cholera: The Biography*, New York: Oxford University Press.

Haufe, C. (2024). *Fruitfulness*, New York: Oxford University Press.

Hempel, C. G. (1945). Studies in the Logic of Confirmation. *Mind*, **54**(213), 1–26.

Intemann, K. (2005). Feminism, Underdetermination, and Values in Science. *Philosophy of Science*, **72**(5), 1001–1012.

Ivanova, M. (2014). Is There a Place for Epistemic Virtues in Theory Choice? In A. Fairweather, ed., *Virtue Epistemology Naturalized*, Cham: Springer, 207–226.

Ivanova, M. (2017). Aesthetic Values in Science. *Philosophy Compass*, **12**(10), e12433.

Ivanova, M. (2021). *Duhem and Holism*, Cambridge: Cambridge University Press.

Keas, M. N. (2018). Systematizing the Theoretical Virtues. *Synthese*, **195**(6), 2761–2793.

Kellert, S. H., Longino, H. E., & Waters, C. K. (eds.). (2006). *Scientific Pluralism*, Minneapolis: University of Minnesota Press.

Kennefick, D. J. (2021). *No Shadow of a Doubt*. Princeton, NJ: Princeton University Press.

Kitcher, P. (1993). *The Advancement of Science*, New York: Oxford University Press.

Kitcher, P. (2001). *Science, Truth, and Democracy*, New York: Oxford University Press.

Kitcher, P. (2012). *Preludes to Pragmatism*, Oxford, New York: Oxford University Press.

Koch, T. (2013). Commentary: Nobody Loves a Critic: Edmund A Parkes and John Snow's Cholera. *International Journal of Epidemiology*, **42**(6), 1553–1559.

Kovaka, K. (2019). Underdetermination and Evidence in the Developmental Plasticity Debate. *British Journal for the Philosophy of Science*, **70**(1), 127–152.

Kuhn, T. S. (1962). *The Structure of Scientific Revolutions*. Chicago: University of Chicago Press,

Kuhn, T. S. (1977). Objectivity, Value Judgment, and Theory Choice. In *The Essential Tension: Selected Studies in Scientific Tradition and Change*, Chicago: University of Chicago Press, 320–339.

Kukla, A. (1996). Does Every Theory Have Empirically Equivalent Rivals? *Erkenntnis*, **44**(2), 137–166.

Kukla, A. (1998). *Studies in Scientific Realism*, New York: Oxford University Press.

Langmuir, A. D. (1961). Epidemiology of Airborne Infection. *Bacteriological Reviews*, **25**(3): 173–181.

Laudan, L. (1977). *Progress and Its Problems*, Berkeley: University of California Press.

Laudan, L. (1990). Demystifying Underdetermination. In C. W. Savage, ed., *Scientific Theories*, Minneapolis: University of Minnesota Press, 267–297.

Laudan, L., & Leplin, J. (1991). Empirical Equivalence and Underdetermination. *The Journal of Philosophy*, **88**(9), 449–472.

Liebig, J. (1842). *Chemistry in Its Application to Agriculture and Physiology*, London: Taylor and Walton.

Longino, H. (1990). *Science as Social Knowledge*, Princeton: Princeton University Press.

Longino, H. (2004). How Values Can Be Good for Science. In P. Machamer & G. Wolters, eds., *Science, Values, and Objectivity*, Pittsburgh: University of Pittsburgh Press, 127–142.

Manchak, J. B. (2009). Can We Know the Global Structure of Spacetime? *Studies in History and Philosophy of Science Part B*, **40**(1), 53–56.

Massimi, M. (2022). *Perspectival Realism*, Oxford: Oxford University Press.

Mayo, D. G. (1997). Severe Tests, Arguing from Error, and Methodological Underdetermination. *Philosophical Studies*, **86**(3), 243–266.

McAllister, J. W. (1999). *Beauty and Revolution in Science*, Ithaca: Cornell University Press.

McMullin, E. (1982). Values in Science. *PSA: Proceedings of the Biennial Meeting of the Philosophy of Science Association*. Cambridge: Cambridge University Press, 3–28.

McMullin, E. (1996). Epistemic Virtue and Theory Appraisal. In I. Douven & L. Horsten, eds., *Realism in the Sciences*, Leuven: Leuven University Press, 13–34.

Miyake, T. (2015). Underdetermination and Decomposition in Kepler's Astronomia Nova. *Studies in History and Philosophy of Science Part A*, **50**, 20–27.

Newton, I. (1966 [1687]). *Philosophiæ Naturalis Principia Mathematica [1687]*. (Motte, Trans.), sixth printing, Berkeley and Los Angeles: University of California.

Okasha, S. (1997). Laudan and Leplin on Empirical Equivalence. *The British Journal for the Philosophy of Science*, **48**(2), 251–256.

Parkes, E. (1855). Mode of Communication of Cholera by John Snow, M. D. 2nd Ed. *British and Foreign Medico-Chirurgical Review*, **15**, 449–463.

Pietsch, W. (2012). Hidden Underdetermination: A Case Study in Classical Electrodynamics. *International Studies in the Philosophy of Science*, **26**(2), 125–151.

Potochnik, A. (2015). The Diverse Aims of Science. *Studies in History and Philosophy of Science Part A*, **53**, 71–80.

Psillos, S. (1999). *Scientific Realism: How Science Tracks Truth*, New York: Routledge.

Quine, W. V. O. (1951). Two Dogmas of Empiricism, *Philosophical Review* **60**(1), 20–43.

Quine, W. V. O. (1975). On Empirically Equivalent Systems of the World. *Erkenntnis*, **9**(3), 313–328.

Schindler, S. (2018). *Theoretical Virtues in Science*, Cambridge: Cambridge University Press.

Snow, J. (1849). *On the Mode of Communication of Cholera* (2nd Ed.), London: John Churchill.

Snow, J. (1851). On the Mode of Propagation of Cholera. *Medical Times*, **24**, 559–562, 610–612.

Snow, J. (1855). *On the Mode of Communication of Cholera*, London: John Churchill.

Snow, J. (1856). Cholera and the Water Supply in the South Districts of London in 1854. *Journal of Public Health, and Sanitary Review*, 239–257.

Sober, E. (1975). *Simplicity*, Oxford: Oxford University Press.

Stanford, P. K. (2006). *Exceeding Our Grasp*, New York: Oxford University Press.

Steel, D. (2010). Epistemic Values and the Argument from Inductive Risk. *Philosophy of Science*, **77**(1), 14–34.

Stegenga, J. (2024). Justifying Scientific Progress. *Philosophy of Science*, **91**, 543–560.

Tulodziecki, D. (2007). Breaking the Ties: Epistemic Significance, Bacilli, and Underdetermination. *Studies in History and Philosophy of Science Part C*, **38**(3), 627–641.

Tulodziecki, D. (2011). A Case Study in Explanatory Power: John Snow's Conclusions about the Pathology and Transmission of Cholera. *Studies in History and Philosophy of Science Part C*, **42**(3), 306–316.

Tulodziecki, D. (2012a). Epistemic Equivalence and Epistemic Incapacitation. *The British Journal for the Philosophy of Science*, **63**(2), 313–328.

Tulodziecki, D. (2012b). Principles of Reasoning in Historical Epidemiology. *Journal of Evaluation in Clinical Practice*, **18**(5), 968–973.

Tulodziecki, D. (2013). Underdetermination, Methodological Practices, and Realism. *Synthese*, **190**(17), 3731–3750.

Tulodziecki, D. (2014). Epistemic Virtues and the Success of Science. In A. Fairweather, ed., *Virtue Epistemology Naturalized*, Vol. 366, Cham: Springer, 247–268.

Tulodziecki, D. (2016a). From Zymes to Germs: Discarding the Realist/Anti-Realist Framework. In T. Sauer & R. Scholl, eds., *The Philosophy of Historical Case Studies*, Vol. 319, Springer, 265–283.

Tulodziecki, D. (2016b). Structural Realism beyond Physics. *Studies in History and Philosophy of Science Part A*, **59**, 106–114.

Tulodziecki, D. (2017a). Abandoning the Realism Debate: Lessons from the Zymotic Theory of Disease. In M. Massimi, J.-W. Romeijn, & G. Schurz, eds., *EPSA15 Selected Papers*, Vol. 5, Springer, 61–69.

Tulodziecki, D. (2017b). Against Selective Realism(s). *Philosophy of Science*, **84**(5), 996–1007.

Tulodziecki, D. (2017c). Underdetermination. In J. Saatsi, ed., *The Routledge Handbook of Scientific Realism*, New York: Routledge, 60–71.

Tulodziecki, D. (2019). How (Not) to Think about Theory-Change in Epidemiology. *Synthese*. **198**, 2569–2588.

Tulodziecki, D. (2021). Virtues in Scientific Practice. In E. Ratti & T. A. Stapleford, eds., *Science, Technology, and Virtues*, Oxford: Oxford University Press, 200–222.

Turner, D. (2005). Local Underdetermination in Historical Science. *Philosophy of Science*, **72**(1), 209–230.

van Fraassen, B. C. (1980). *The Scientific Image*, New York: Oxford University Press.

Van Fraassen, B. C. (1984). Empiricism in the Philosophy of Science. In P. M. Churchland & C. A. Hooker, eds., *Images of Science*, Chicago: University of Chicago Press, 245–308.

Vinten-Johansen, P., Brody, H., Paneth, N., Rachman, S., Rip, M. and Zuck, D. (2003). *Cholera, Chloroform, and the Science of Medicine*, Oxford: Oxford University Press.

Wegener, A. (1915). *Die Entstehung der Kontinente und Ozeane*, Braunschweig: Vieweg & Sohn.

Worboys, M. (2000). *Spreading Germs*, Cambridge: Cambridge University Press.

Worrall, J. (1989). Fresnel, Poisson and the White Spot: The Role of Successful Predictions in the Acceptance of Scientific Theories. In D. Gooding, T. Pinch, & S. Schaffer, eds., *The Uses of Experiment*, Cambridge, Cambridge University Press, 135–158.

Acknowledgements

Many thanks to Matthias Egg, Uljana Feest, Chris Haufe, Lydia Patton, Marshall Porterfield, and the referees for helpful points and discussions. Special thanks to Jacob Stegenga for his support, to Martin Curd for commenting on a draft, and to the late Hank Frankel for many conversations about continental drift and HPS. This project was supported by Purdue University's "Elevating the Visibility of Research: Seed Funding for Academic Books and Monographs (2024)" through the Office of Research and by the Purdue University Books Initiative through the Office of the Provost.

Cambridge Elements

Philosophy of Science

Jacob Stegenga
NTU Singapore

Jacob Stegenga is a Professor at NTU Singapore, and previously taught at the University of Cambridge. He has published widely in philosophy of science and philosophy of medicine, and is the author of *Medical Nihilism*, described as 'a landmark work', *Care and Cure: An Introduction to Philosophy of Medicine*, and a book to be published in 2025 titled *Heart of Science*.

About the Series

This series of Elements in Philosophy of Science provides an extensive overview of the themes, topics and debates which constitute the philosophy of science. Distinguished specialists provide an up-to-date summary of the results of current research on their topics, as well as offering their own take on those topics and drawing original conclusions.

Cambridge Elements

Philosophy of Science

Elements in the Series

Scientific Progress
Darrell P. Rowbottom

Modelling Scientific Communities
Cailin O'Connor

Logical Empiricism as Scientific Philosophy
Alan W. Richardson

Scientific Models and Decision Making
Eric Winsberg and Stephanie Harvard

Science and the Public
Angela Potochnik

Feminist Philosophy of Science
Anke Bueter

Abductive Reasoning in Science
Finnur Dellsén

Climate Science
Wendy S. Parker

The Social Dimensions of Scientific Knowledge: Consensus, Controversy, and Coproduction
Boaz Miller

Scientific Realism
Timothy D. Lyons

Science, Pseudoscience, and the Demarcation Problem
Dániel Bárdos and Adam Tamas Tuboly

Underdetermination and Theoretical Virtues
Dana Tulodziecki

A full series listing is available at: www.cambridge.org/EPSC

For EU product safety concerns, contact us at Calle de José Abascal, 56–1°,
28003 Madrid, Spain or eugpsr@cambridge.org.

www.ingramcontent.com/pod-product-compliance
Ingram Content Group UK Ltd.
Pitfield, Milton Keynes, MK11 3LW, UK
UKHW031426300625
460082UK00018B/254